Your Bible
Your Destiny

Billy Lambert

Billy Lambert
15665 Daugherty Road
Foley, Alabama 36535

© 2012 Billy Lambert

Scripture quotations from New King
James Version unless otherwise indicated.

Printed in the United States of America

ISBN: 9780615598420

To the Memory
of
My Dear Grandson

Caleb B. Coxwell

July 9, 1998–July 15, 2009

My Grandson

Caleb was a very unusual young man. At age six he informed me, "Granddaddy, I want to do something to help the church." He left the room, came back with the pictorial church directory, and began pointing to the pictures of those who had been absent from worship. He then telephoned them. Soon the whole congregation knew—if you miss, Caleb will call you.

A few weeks before that fateful Wednesday, Caleb approached me: "Granddaddy, I want to talk about being a preacher."

"Do you really want to preach?" I gently quizzed him.

His response was firm. "Yes!"

I assured him that I would help him as much as possible. I promised him my library.

Later that week, Caleb strolled into the den and observed my putting the finishing touches on the evening class I was to teach. "I am going to write a sermon," he proclaimed.

"If you do, you may extend the invitation tonight," I promised.

He got busy, and without help from Granddaddy he prepared a short outline entitled, "Wearing Down Our Spiritual Life." It was not perfect but rather outstanding for a ten-year-old. (See Caleb's unedited sermon on page 157.)

A short time later, a fellow preacher put that outline on a church Website. Yes, Caleb preached it again. And he is still preaching it by computer, by the printed page, and by the example he set. "He being dead yet speaketh" (Hebrews 11:4 KJV).

Caleb was making plans to attend Faulkner University in Montgomery, Alabama, to prepare to peach the gospel. He had told me, "I am going to take your place one day."

He died tragically. Not a day goes by that I don't think about him. He is forever in my heart.

Billy Lambert

Contents

Introduction

The sermons in this book were preached in gospel meetings and in local work at the Summerdale Church of Christ. V. P. Black and Jimmy Faulkner, Sr., friends of mine, had encouraged me to publish a volume of sermons. After much hesitation, I have decided to do so.

The death of my grandson, Caleb Benjamin Coxwell, on July 15, 2009, prompted me to give serious consideration to this project. You now hold in your hands, the result of brother Black's and brother Faulkner's encouragement, and especially, the effects of Caleb's death on my life.

Billy Lambert
February 2, 2012

1

A Thousand Years from Now

But the heavens and the earth which are now preserved by the same word, are reserved for fire until the day of judgment and perdition of ungodly men. But, beloved, do not forget this one thing, that with the Lord one day is as a thousand years, and a thousand years as one day. The Lord is not slack concerning His promise, as some count slackness, but is longsuffering toward us, not willing that any should perish but that all should come to repentance. But the day of the Lord will come as a thief in the night, in which the heavens will pass away with a great noise, and the elements will melt with fervent heat; both the earth and the works that are in it will be burned up. Therefore, since all these things will be dissolved, what manner of persons ought you to be in holy conduct and godliness (2 Peter 3:7–11).

We calculate it in seconds, minutes, hours, days, weeks, years, decades, centuries, and millenniums, but with God time has no significance. He does not need to measure time. Isaiah explains why. "For thus says the High and Lofty One Who inhabits eternity" (Isaiah 57:15). God is timeless because He inhabits eternity.

One thing is sure: our time is short. The Bible says, "The days of our lives are seventy years; and if by reason of strength they are eighty years, yet their boast is only labor and sorrow." Why? "For it is soon cut off, and we fly away." (Psalm 90:10). Verse 12 says, "So teach us to number our days, that we may gain a heart of wisdom."

The Bible also says our days are "swifter than a weaver's shuttle" (Job 7:6) and our life is like water spilled on the ground or steam above the kettle: "It is even a vapor that appears for a little time and then vanishes away" (James 4:14). Life is short.

We can do without some things, but none of us can do without time. When our time is gone, our life ends. Thomas Edison said, "Time is the most important thing in the world." Benjamin Franklin said, "Dost thou love life? Then do not squander time, for time is the stuff of which life is made."

Our time on earth is limited. God does not calculate our lives like we do. With God, "one day is as a thousand years." I do not understand that. With God, "a thousand years is as one day." I know that is true, but I don't understand that either. Things that really concern us now are temporal. In a thousand years it is not going to matter if you had the maximum education from every college and university in America or if you could barely write your name. A thousand years from now it will not matter if you drove the finest automobile that money could buy or if you had to hire a taxi or ask a friend for a ride. A thousand years from now it will not matter if you wore the finest clothes, nicest suits, or latest-fashion dresses or if you bought your clothes at bargain basement yard sales. A thousand years from now it won't matter if you were a world traveler or never left your hometown. A thousand years from now it will not matter if you ate the finest food or barely had enough to eat from one day to the next.

What Shall I Do with Jesus?

But what about other things—spiritual decisions? A thousand years from now they will matter. Pilate said, "What then shall I do with Jesus who is called Christ?" (Matthew 27:22). It will matter in a thousand years what you did with Him, what Pilate did with Him, and what the world did with Him.

Revelation 14:13 says, "Blessed are the dead who die in the Lord from now on. 'Yes,' says the Spirit, 'that they may rest from their labors, and their works follow them.'" It will matter whether or not you died in the Lord. So I know what we can do with Christ. We can accept Him on the terms of His will. He said, "Why do you call me 'Lord, Lord' and do not do the things that I say?" (Luke 6:46). Lordship and obedience go together. We have no right to call Him Lord unless we are willing to obey Him. So we can either accept Him on the terms of His will or reject Him. We will do one or the other. Jesus said, "You are not willing to come to Me that you may have life" (John 5:40). They rejected Him. It really is going to matter in a thousand years what we did with Jesus.

Am I Spiritual?

Right now it matters what you do with Him in your personal life. Do you have peace of mind, forgiveness of sins, and freedom from guilt? It matters right now! It is going to matter in eternity what you do now with Jesus Christ.

A thousand years from today it will matter what you have done to deepen your spiritual life. Some charge that there is a lack of spirituality in the church. I do not know whether or not that is true. But here is what I do know. The apostle Paul, "For to be carnally minded is death, but to be spiritually minded is life and peace" (Romans 8:6). If I am worldly, carnally, and fleshly minded, I am focused on material things, and that is going to matter in a thousand years. What are we doing to deepen our spiritual lives? How can we do that?

I highly recommend that you include the fruit of the Spirit in your life. You must do so if you want to deepen your spirituality. If you do not want to be just a superficial Christian, include the fruit of the Spirit. Galatians 5:22–23 describes this fruit. "But the fruit of the Spirit is love, joy, peace, longsuffering, kindness, goodness, faithfulness, gentleness, self-control. Against such there is no law." I know I am spiritual if I reflect these characteristics.

Spiritual Fruit

What is the fruit of the Spirit? Love is foundational. First we are to love God with all our heart, soul, mind, and strength. We are also to love our neighbor, our fellow man, and our brethren. We are to love even our enemies. Are you known as an individual of love?

Joy is evidence that we are Christ's. What kind of person are you? Do you brighten a room when you enter or when you leave?

Consider love, joy, and peace. First, we need inner peace. We also need to be at peace with God through Christ (Romans 5:1; Colossians 1:20). Then we need to be "peaceable" people, following after things that show peace. How do your daily contacts feel about you? Do they have trouble getting along with you?

Another spiritual quality is goodness—just plain, old-fashioned goodness. The Bible says, "The steps of a good man are ordered by the Lord" (Psalm 37:23).

Gentleness also gives spiritual depth. Second Timothy 2:24 says, "And a servant of the Lord must not quarrel but be gentle to all, able to teach, patient." Are you a gentle person?

Then Paul mentions faith. How strong is your faith? How deep is it? Is it strong enough to support you in life and comfort you in death?

What about your self-control—temperance? Paul evidently had a personal struggle with that one. He said, "O wretched man that I am! Who will deliver me from this body of death" (Romans 7:24). The answer to the question is Christ. Look at 1 Corinthians 9:27: "I discipline my body and bring it into subjection, lest, when I have preached to others, I myself should become disqualified." What is he talking about? Self-control!

Do I Love the Church?

What are we doing to strengthen our spiritual lives? It does matter, you know. It matters now and it will always matter. A thousand years from now it will matter what you have done with the church. Jesus loved the church and He gave Himself for it (Ephesians 5:25). I can never be like Jesus if I do not love what Jesus loved. He loved the church; He died for it!

What does His church mean to you? Most people today who call themselves Christians perceive the church as absolutely meaningless. God means nothing to them. Jesus means nothing to them. The Bible means nothing to them. Salvation means nothing to them. Something is terribly wrong when a member of the church of Christ does not put the church first in his or her life.

How can I show my love for the church? One way is by living right—plain old living right. This is done by being a good example for others to follow. Philippians 1:27 reads, "Only let your conduct be worthy of the gospel of Christ." My life needs to be worthy of the gospel. It needs to be in harmony with the gospel. I can show my love for the church by being zealous in the work of the church. I need to be on fire!

> After a gospel message, several wayward church members responded to the invitation of Christ to be restored to their fellowship with Christ and His church. One woman was "up in her years." She really did not know what to say because this was a first-time experience. She listened as the preacher spoke with other respondents. The preacher asked each, "Why did you come forward?" The responses were something like, "I've been doing so and so, and I am going to quit." So when the preacher came to her and asked, "Sister, why did you come forward?" she replied, "Preacher, I ain't been doin' nothin', and I'm gonna quit."

Also, we can show our love for the church by our excited involvement. Jesus was zeal personified. He said, "I must work the works of Him who sent Me while it is day; the night is coming when no one can work" (John 9:4). The time is coming when neither you nor I will be able to work for the Lord.

What are we doing with the church? It is going to matter in a thousand years.

My Sin

A thousand years from now it will matter what I have done with my sin. That sounds easy but I know what can happen. Sometimes we try to blame sin on someone else as King Saul did. We try to hide our sins as Adam and Eve did in the Garden of Eden. We try to hide from God. Job 34:22 says, "There is no darkness nor shadow of death where the workers of iniquity may hide themselves." There is just no place where we can do that.

Sometimes we try to "whitewash" our sins. Some of you may not know about whitewashing, so I'll explain. When I was a boy, my job was to whitewash the trees in the yard. I painted their trunks from the ground up to about four feet. How magnificent our yard looked. But it took only one good rain to return the beautiful yard to dull. So as soon as the sun came out, I returned to the brown trunks with my brush and whitewash to do that job all over again.

Whitewash your life all you like, but your sins remain underneath, temporarily hidden. Proverbs 28:13 says, "He who covers his sins will not prosper, but whoever confesses and forsakes them will have mercy."

What can I do with my sins? I can have them forgiven. Psalm 32:1 says, "Blessed is he whose transgression is forgiven, whose sin is covered." The only way I can really be happy is to know that the Lord has forgiven my sin. That happens when I come in contact with the blood of the Lord Jesus Christ. Colossians 2:11 talks about the circumcision made without hands—the circumcision of the heart. In verse 12, Paul discusses how that circumcision takes place. God cuts away the sins of our hearts when we are buried with Him in baptism. Then we are risen with Him through the faith in the operation of God (Colossians 2:12). God does the operating.

So you say, "Bother Lambert, I've already done that. I have been a member of the church for years, but I know that I have not done everything I should have." I've stood many times at the door after worship to greet members following worship only to hear many say, "I thought about responding this morning." (I am talking about members of the church of Christ.) But they didn't respond, and it did not take them long to forget the tug of the gospel on their heart.

So what do I need to do? Read 1 John 1:9. It was written for Christians. "If we confess our sins, He is faithful and just to forgive us our sins." Do Christians sin? Of course! If we were perfect we would not need Jesus. If we were perfect we would not need His blood. And if a Christian sins, he does not need to be baptized again. He needs to confess his sin and ask God's forgiveness. If that sin is private, he needs to go into his closet and talk to God about it. If it is public, then he need to confess it publicly.

What are we doing with our sins? It is going to matter in a thousand years.

Warnings

A thousand years from now it will matter what you have done with the warnings of God. God warns the unsaved in a number of ways. "Do not boast about tomorrow, for you do not know what a day may bring forth" (Proverbs 27:1). What about Amos 4:12? "Prepare to meet your God." God warns us. He warns the backslider in Matthew 25:13. "Watch therefore, for you know neither the day nor the hour in which the Son of man is coming." We want to be prepared. We want to be ready. We want to know that we are prepared. We want to know that we are ready when the bridegroom comes.

When the Titanic sank, more than fifteen hundred lives were lost—some women, some children, and most of the men aboard. Here is what is so sad. The captain was warned of icebergs ahead, but he did not heed the warning. After all, his vessel was unsinkable—at least, he thought so.

What are we doing with God's warnings? Are we ignoring them? Are we listening to Him? In a thousand years it will matter what you have done with the warnings of God.

What Matters

Remember this: Some things matter now! It matters now what you do with Jesus. It matters now what you are doing with your spiritual life. It matters now what you are doing with the church. It matters now what you are doing with your sins, the Word of God, and the warnings of God. It matters. All of these actions matter now!

SERMON

2

The Unknown God

"For as I was passing through and considering the objects of your worship, I even found an altar with this inscription: TO THE UNKNOWN GOD. Therefore, the One whom you worship without knowing, Him I proclaim to you: God, who made the world and everything in it, since He is Lord of heaven and earth, does not dwell in temples made with hands. Nor is He worshiped with men's hands, as though He needed anything, since He gives to all life, breath, and all things. And He has made from one blood every nation of men to dwell on all the face of the earth, and has determined their preappointed times and the boundaries of their dwellings, so that they should seek the Lord, in the hope that they might grope for Him and find Him, though He is not far from each one of us; for in Him we live and move and have our being, as also some of your own poets have said, 'For we are also His offspring.' Therefore, since we are the offspring of God, we ought not to think that the Divine Nature is like gold or silver or stone, something shaped by art and man's devising. Truly, these times of ignorance God overlooked, but now commands all men everywhere to repent, because He has appointed a day on which He will judge the world in righteousness by the Man whom He has ordained. He has given assurance of this to all by raising Him from the dead." And when they heard of the resurrection of the dead, some mocked, while others said, "We will hear you again on this matter." So Paul departed from among them. However, some men joined him and believed, among them Dionysius the Areopagite, a woman named Damaris, and others with them. (Acts 17:23–34).

When an angry mob drove Paul out of Thessalonica, he went to Berea. The people there were receptive to the gospel (Acts

17:10–11). The persecuting Jews of Thessalonica followed Paul to Berea and there stirred up the people. Paul then left Berea and came to Athens. As he waited there for Timothy and Silas, he had opportunity to preach to the men of Athens.

Athens was the most celebrated city of Greece. Founded some sixteen hundred years before the Christian Age, it was distinguished for its military talent, learning, eloquence, luxury, and politeness of its citizens. No city of antiquity was so celebrated for its warriors, statesmen, philosophers, sculptors, and poets. On every side were temples and altars. Among those was an altar with a peculiar inscription: *To the Unknown God.*

Paul's spirit stirred with jealousy for the true God when he witnessed the idolatry in Athens. Every idol and every altar was a public dishonor to the true God. It provoked him with compassionate indignation for the Athenians—compassion for the idolater, and indignation for the idol. It motivated him with intense anxiety for their welfare and salvation. Athens was the seat of Satan. They were under his spell.

The Acropolis, the glory of Grecian art, held deposits of the most interesting in painting, sculpture, and architecture in Athens, as well as serving as a home for the Parthenon. Measuring 217 feet in length and 98 feet in width, that magnificent building contained a statue of Minerva, a masterpiece of art of ivory, 39 feet tall and covered with pure gold. Three-quarters of a mile north of the town was the academy where Plato taught and the Lyceum where Aristotle diffused the light of science. In the center of Athens, a rocky formation called the Areopagus rose above the surrounding landscape and provided a place for the court of the supreme judges, who enforced justice and dispensed Athenian laws, to meet. They held court after midnight so as not to be distracted. Citizens of that highly educated city were given to idolatry.

Paul Contended with Religious Leaders

Paul disputed with the Jews in the synagogue, with devout persons on the street, and with vendors and buyers in the market (Acts 17:17). He was opposed by the Epicureans and the Stoics (Acts 17:18). Epicurus, founder of the sect, flourished about three hundred years before Christ. Since his main tenet was pleasure as the chief good, his followers were given to idolatry, effeminacy, and voluptuousness.

The Stoics were a sect of philosophers. They believed in only one Supreme Being. They also believed all things happen by fatal necessity. They further held that happiness comes by being totally insensitive to pain.

As Paul came to the seat of idolatrous worship, he could not keep quiet. He perceived that they were "too superstitious" (Acts 17:22 KJV). They had gone to the extreme. The city was full of idols, temples, and altars. One historian said it was easier to find a god in Athens than to find a man.

The Unknown God

The Athenians added a place of sacrifice for a generic god to make sure they left none out. That altar's inscription was: *To the Unknown God*. The true God was unknown to them. It is sad—yea, tragic—when men and women do not know God. "The wicked in his proud countenance does not seek God; God is in none of his thoughts" (Psalm 10:4).

> And to give you who are troubled rest with us when the Lord Jesus is revealed from heaven with His mighty angels, in flaming fire taking vengeance on those who do not know God, and on those who do not obey the gospel of our Lord Jesus Christ. These shall be punished with everlasting destruction from the presence of the Lord and from the glory of His power (2 Thessalonians 1:7–9).

Note Paul's defense of God from Acts 17:23–28:

- *Paul proclaims God as the one true God.* He declares Him to be the creator of all things (vv. 23–24).

- *Paul declares His dominion and authority.* "He is Lord of heaven and earth" (v. 24).

- *Paul declares the immensity of His nature.* He "does not dwell in temples made with hands" (v. 24).

- *Paul declares God as the self-existent one and the source of all life.* "Nor is He worshiped with men's hands as though He needed anything, since He gives to all life, breath, and all things" (v. 25).

- *Paul recognizes God as the universal parent of mankind.* "And He has made from one blood every nation of men to dwell on all the face of the earth" (v. 26).

- *Paul declares God to be the ruler and disposer of all events.* "And has determined their preappointed times and the boundaries of their dwellings" (v. 26).

- *Paul declares God as an omnipresent being.* "He is not far from each one of us" (v. 27).

- *Paul proclaims God as the source of all our possessions.* "For in Him we live and move and have our being" (v. 28).

- *Paul declares God's spiritual nature.* "Since we are the offspring of God, we ought not to think that the Divine Nature is like gold or silver or stone, something shaped by art and man's devising" (v. 29).

Man is the crowning work in God's creation having been made in the image of God (Genesis 1:26–27).

The Prescription

Paul presented a remedy for the heathen world that, by their idol worship, declared themselves ignorant of the true God. "Truly, these times of ignorance God overlooked, but now commands all men everywhere to repent" (Acts 17:30). Repentance is not an option. It is a divine necessity (Luke 13:3).

Men should repent and turn to God "because He has appointed a day on which He will judge the world in righteousness" (Acts 17:31).

- The judgment will be universal involving the "world," that is, all men (Acts 17:31).

- God will mete out judgment on an individual basis. All must give an account to God (Romans 2:12; 14:12; John 12:48).

- Paul told the Athenians that God will judge the world in "righteousness" (Acts 17:31).

- The psalmist declares God's commandments to be righteousness (Psalm 119:172).

- We cannot be made righteous without obeying God's commands (Romans 6:1–7, 17–18).

Knowing the terror of the Lord (2 Corinthians 5:11), I urge you to obey God's commands. Believe Jesus, His Son (John 8:24); repent of your sins (Luke 13:3); confess faith in Christ (Romans 10:9–10); and be baptized (immersed) into Christ (Galatians 3:27) so He will add you to His family, His church (cf. Ephesians 3:15; Acts 2:47).

The Postponement

The audience offered mixed reactions to Paul's sermon. There was denial. Some in Paul's audience mocked, just as some did on the day of Pentecost (Acts 2:13). Some procrastinated: "We will hear you again on this matter" (Acts 17:32). Felix reacted the same way when Paul preached to him: "Go away for now; when I have a convenient time I will call for you" (Acts 24:25).

The worst mistake one can make is to delay making a positive decision about Christ.

The Pardon

"Some men joined him and believed" (Acts 17:34). Among those who believed was Dionysus, who is thought to have been a person of some reputation in Athens. Another believer was a woman named Damaris. These turned from their idol worship to serve a living God (1 Thessalonians 1:9).

Is our world so different from the world of Paul's day? All men are in need of Jesus. May we all pray that our unbelieving world of the twenty-first century will heed the clarion call of the gospel of Christ!

3

Spiritual Cancer

A man was overheard in a doctor's office saying, "I earn fifty thousand dollars a year, and I give eight dollars every time I go to church." He was soul-sick and unaware of it.

Covetousness is a spiritual cancer that eats away at the soul of a man. Few people are free from the taint of this sin. Even people who say they love the Lord are guilty of this sin.

Because from the least of them even to the greatest of them, everyone is given to covetousness; and from the prophet even to the priest, everyone deals falsely (Jeremiah 6:13).

> So they come to you as people do, they sit before you as My people, and they hear your words, but they do not do them; for with their mouth they show much love, but their hearts pursue their own gain (Ezekiel 33:31).

The last of the Ten Commandments was, "Thou shalt not covet" (Exodus 20:17 KJV). Achan broke this commandment just before Israel's attack on Ai (Joshua 7). That small city should have fallen easily into the hands of the Israelites as did Jericho. However, God had previously forbidden anyone to take any of the spoils of Jericho (Joshua 6:17–21). With Israel's defeat at Ai, God revealed there was sin in camp. The guilty man was Achan. He coveted the spoils and hid them in his tent. As a result, he, his family members, and his animals were stoned to death. The stolen goods, his tent, and other possessions were added to the dead bodies in the Valley of Achor and burned. Then they were buried and covered with stones.

Covetousness means "to fix the desire upon . . . whether things good or bad." It can also mean, "to lust after"; "a desire to have more." The word is used to describe "money-loving" (Luke 16:14; 2 Timothy 3:2).

All covetousness is not sinful. "But covet earnestly the best gifts" (1 Corinthians 12:31 KJV). Paul also wrote, "covet to prophesy" (1 Corinthians 14:39 KJV).

When Covetousness is Sin

Yet there is a covetous spirit that is sinful. Significantly, Paul couples this covetousness with the most loathsome sins (Ephesians 5:5). A covetous man is an idolater because he loves, trusts, and serves money more than God (Matthew 6:24). Covetousness is a subtle sin. It transforms itself into an angel of light and calls itself *prudence, thrift,* and other deceptive names. It wears a cloak to conceal its true nature (1 Thessalonians 2:5).

- *Covetousness is a root sin.* Love of money is the root of all evil (1 Timothy 6:10). It is a sin that hinders God's Word (Luke 8:14). Covetousness caused Ananias and Sapphira to lie about their giving (Acts 5:1–5). This sin is worthy of censure (1 Corinthians 5:9–10) because it can cause the loss of the soul of man (Ephesians 5:5).

- *Covetousness is a heart problem.* It issues forth from the heart (Mark 7:21–22); it is greed for the things of this world (Luke 12:15). This heart malady brings trouble to a man's house (Proverbs 15:27). Our lives should be void of covetousness (Hebrews 13:5).

- *Covetousness is not satisfying.* The covetous always want more. Solomon wrote, "He who loves silver will not be satisfied with silver; nor he who loves abundance, with increase" (Ecclesiastes 5:10). Someone once said, "How strange it is that when men get rich, they are just as unsatisfied and anxious to make money as when they were poor."

- *Covetousness is injurious.* It drowns men in perdition (1 Timothy 6:9).

A number of years ago, the ship *Kent* was bound from England to the East Indies. During the voyage, she caught fire. Another vessel came along side it to rescue passengers and crew. The sea was extremely rough, tossing about the small rescue vessels like corks. One of the crewmen on the stricken ship knew that a mate had a large amount of gold, so he broke into his mate's cabin, filled his belt with as many pieces as it would hold, and strapped it around his waist. Then he slipped down the rope toward a little boat below. A sudden movement of the waves caused the boat to move, and the crewman plunged into the sea. Although he was a good swimmer, he could not overcome the extra weight around his waist. He sank to the ocean floor. That which he coveted proved to be his downfall.

Industries of Covetousness

William Barclay, in *The Ten Commandments for Today,* said, "The simplest form of covetousness is covetousness of material things, covetousness for money and the things which money can buy" (p. 199). The gambling craze is based on the desire to get money, even at the expense of others.

The movie industry's foundation is based on the desire to get money, even if filth and garbage must be used to obtain it. The alcohol industry is based on greed. The broken homes, destroyed lives, and crimes generated from beverage alcohol are inconsequential to those bent on making bucks from booze.

Will a Man Rob God?

Covetousness can turn a man into a monster. Covetousness is such an overmastering desire for what belongs to another that the laws of right and justice are violated to obtain it.

When a man covets his neighbor's property, his desire is disgraceful (Exodus 20:17). It is also disgraceful when a man covets that which belongs to God who owns everything (Psalm 24:1; 50:10–12; Haggai 2:8; Ezekiel 18:4; 1 Corinthians 6:19–20). When men refuse to give as they have prospered, they are coveting what is God's. When covetousness takes hold, it turns an honest man into a thief (Malachi 3:8–10). There are many reasons men rob God, but at the top of the list is covetousness.

Overcome Covetousness

- *Recognize the ownership of God* (1 Chronicles 29:11). We own nothing; He owns all.

- *Recognize the transitory nature of life* (1 Timothy 6:6–8). We came into the world empty-handed and we will leave the same way. Alexander the Great gave orders that at his death, his hands be left hanging out of his coffin so men would see he carried nothing with him.

- *Realize that the only treasures we keep are those that are laid up in heaven* (Matthew 6:19–21). Giving liberally on the Lord's day will help fight the destructive spiritual malady of covetousness (1 Corinthians 16:1–2).

We do not have a lack of money in the Lord's church. If you believe to the contrary, take a look at the automobiles in the parking lot on Sunday. And then look at our houses. Our problem is desire. When our desire that men be saved grows intense enough, we will be loosed from the shackles of covetousness and will give in order that all men might learn the saving message of the cross.

SERMON

4

Give Us a Little Reviving

And now for a little space grace hath been shewed from the Lord our God, to leave us a remnant to escape, and to give us a nail in his holy place, that our God may lighten our eyes, and give us a little reviving in our bondage (Ezra 9:8; KJV).

My prayer for the church all over the world is that our God will give us a little reviving. The words of our text were spoken some 450 years before our Lord Jesus Christ walked this earth.

The book of 2 Kings ends with Babylon's captivity of God's people. During that captivity, Jeremiah and Ezekiel prophesied about Judah's return to Jerusalem. In Jeremiah 29:10, the prophet predicted that after seventy years God would visit his people and cause them to return to their homeland. When Cyrus came to power near the end of that seventy-year period, he issued an edict that allowed Judah to return to their homeland.

Zerubbabel led more than forty thousand Jews to Jerusalem to rebuild the temple and to establish normal life there. The temple that was eventually built was rather plain in comparison to Solomon's temple that Nebuchadnezzar had destroyed in 586 BC.

Sixty years after Zerubbabel pioneered the first wave of returnees to Jerusalem, Ezra was sent to Jerusalem to restore that law of God. Upon arriving, he was "astonished" (Ezra 9:4). God's people were neglecting the law of God. They had begun to intermarry with the pagans. Ezra was heartbroken, so heartbroken that he tore his own mantel and garments.

The tearing of garments indicated personal grief, and tearing mantels indicated grief representative of the people. Ezra then plucked out the hair of his head and beard and fell on his face before God. He prayed, no doubt with tears coursing his cheeks: "Oh, God, give us a little reviving."

That is still an appropriate prayer in our times, is it not? May the God of heaven give us reviving in these days. Some may say, "Well, preacher, you're beside yourself. Why should we even be concerned about a little reviving in our time?"

Bible Examples in Need of Reviving

We may not be nearly as well off as we think. Who in the Bible had this problem?

- *The Pharisees.* On the outside they looked like whitewashed tombs, but on the inside, they were "full dead men's bones and all uncleanness" (Matthew 23:27). They were not nearly as well off as they thought.

- *The church at Sardis.* Their name indicated they were alive, and yet they were dead, according to Revelation 3:1. The church at Sardis was like an artificial flower; they looked alive but were not. The church was like a life-like department store mannequin. It appeared very normal, but there was no life in it. They were not nearly as well off as they thought.

- *The church at Laodicea.* The Lord said, "I know your works, that you are neither cold nor hot. I could wish that you were cold or hot. So then, because you are lukewarm . . . I will vomit you out of My mouth." Why did the Laodicea church make the Lord nauseated? Because they exhibited this attitude, "I am rich, have become wealthy, and have need of nothing." However, Christ said they were ignorant, that they were really "wretched, miserable, poor, blind, and naked" (Revelation 3:14–17). They were not nearly as well off as they thought.

Christians Today in Need of Reviving

Some in the church of Christ have been subnormal in their Christian lives for so long that if they were to become normal, they would think themselves abnormal. We may not be nearly as well off in God's sight as we think we are. And God knows the true picture.

First Samuel 16:7 tells us that man looks at the outward appearance, but God looks at the heart. The following illustration brings this point home:

> A man spent the better part of a night in a dimly lit, smoke-filled roadhouse, drinking into the wee hours of the morning. As the dawn was breaking, he stepped outside, took a whiff of the fresh air, and said, "What is that smell?" If we were to get a good whiff of pure New Testament Christianity, we too, would wonder, "What in the world is that I smell?"

We may not be nearly as well off as we think. It is hard for us to see ourselves as others see us and as God sees us.

That reminds me of a story of the grandfather who fell sleep on the sofa. His grandchildren decided they would rub Limburger cheese in his mustache. He woke up, shook his head, and said, "What is that I smell? This room stinks!" So he walked out onto the front porch, took another good whiff and remarked, "The whole world stinks!" Since most of us have not trained ourselves to be objective, we often think our problems belong to someone else.

Forgetting Is Easy

Another reason we need to ask God to "give us a little reviving" is because we tend to forget our relationship with God. Do you remember the day you obeyed the gospel? Did you walk down an aisle in a gospel meeting? Or maybe it was a tent meeting somewhere. Do you remember the fervor, the zeal, and the enthusiasm in your heart that day? Now, be honest. Do you still feel the same way, or has something happened to that zeal over the years? It is easy to forget, is it not? Peter warns us about being "shortsighted, even to blindness" (2 Peter 1:9). Have we forgotten that we were cleansed from our old sins? It is easy to forget what the Lord has done for us and to drift away from Him.

Urgent Material Things or Important Spiritual Things

Another reason we need to pray for reviving is because it is easy for us to get involved in life's material blessings and lose focus on spiritual things. Jesus warned, "Take heed and beware of covetousness. For one's life does not consist in the abundance of the things he possesses" (Luke 12:15). You see, our life really is not composed of automobiles, houses, or stocks and bonds. Life is composed of things of real value. These are the things that have some redemptive value. But it is easy to get off track. Lord, please Lord, give us a little reviving.

Benefits of Revival

1. *Revival will cause us to become what God wants us to be.* We are not talking about what the preacher wants us to be, what the elders want us to be, what a brotherhood publication wants us to be, or what a some school wants us to be. We are talking about becoming what God wants us to be. And God wants us to be active, alive, and awake.

   Have you ever thought about this? Every figure of God's church in the Bible pictures it alive, awake, and active.

   - *We are to be lights shining.* "Let your light so shine before men, that they may see your good works and glorify your Father in heaven" (Matt. 5:16).
   - *We are to be salt saving.* "You are the salt of the earth; but if the salt loses its flavor, how shall it be seasoned? It is good for nothing but to be thrown out and trampled underfoot by men" (Matt. 5:13).
   - *We are to be branches bearing.* "By this My Father is glorified, that you bear much fruit; so you will be My disciples" (John 15:8).
   - *We are to be an army fighting.* "Fight the good fight of faith, lay hold on eternal life" (1 Timothy 6:12).
   - *We are to be a body serving.* "From whom the whole body, joined and knit together by what every joint supplies, according to the effective working by which every part does its share, causes growth of the body for the edifying of itself in love" (Ephesians 4:16). This simply means

that every member of the body has a place and a function. We are to take our place and to serve in the body of Christ, alive, awake, and active.

2. *Revival will make us more like Jesus, more Christ-like.* Philippians 2:5 says, "Let this mind be in you which was also in Christ Jesus." Romans 8:9 says, "Now if anyone does not have the Spirit of Christ, he is not His." We are to have the Spirit of Christ, the mind of Christ, the attitude of Christ, the disposition of Christ.

Someone may ask, "Well, Brother Lambert, don't you think doctrine is important?" Of course I believe doctrine is important. Second John 9 reads, "Whosoever transgresses and does not abide in the doctrine of Christ does not have God. He who abides in the doctrine of Christ has both the Father and the Son." Though it is important to have the doctrine of Christ, is it not also important to have the mind of Christ? We need to have the attitude of the Lord Jesus Christ. I will go a step beyond that. It is as much the doctrine of Christ to be like Christ as it is to partake of the Lord's supper. And when we have this revival, it will make us more like the Lord Jesus Christ. We will have His mind and His attitude. He had a mind of love, an attitude of forgiveness, mercy, and compassion. It will make us like Christ.

3. *Revival will get the church of Christ in America back into the soul-saving business.* We have left that business, haven't we? Let us be honest. Many of us are like the old lady who said she was so busy doing church work that she didn't have time to save souls. Pray tell, what do we think the work of the church is if it is not to save souls?

> About twenty-two years ago, the late W. B. West, who served as dean of the Harding Graduate School, and later, dean of the Bible department at Faulkner University, asked me to teach a course on "The Preacher and His Work." Later, Brother West took me out to lunch. (I had already learned that when a preacher takes someone to lunch, the guest had better be on guard because the host wants something.)

"Brother Lambert, I'd like for you to teach another class."

I wasn't surprised. "What would you like for me to teach, Brother West?"

"Missions."

"Well, just exactly where would you like for me to begin?" I asked. Brother West was one of the kindest men I have ever known, a true gentleman and a genuine Christian. I assumed I would have a book or syllabus.

So in all his kindness he replied, "Brother Lambert, you might begin with the Great Commission."

Isn't it true that churches of Christ all over the nation should begin with the Great Commission? That is what praying this prayer will do for us. We will become soul winners for Christ. It is easy to get side-tracked and spend a lot of time with good things in the church that do not win souls, when winning souls should be our objective.

You may be thinking, "Well, Brother Lambert, I'm not sure I know enough. We should leave that work to professionals."

Some of the greatest soul winners in the church do not know the difference in an adverb and an adenoid. But they know the gospel plan of salvation, and they want to share that with everyone. A revival will get us back into the business of saving souls, because that business is not a matter of knowledge. It is a matter of loving God and loving people.

I invited a deacon to make a visit with me one night. When we arrived at the house, no one was home. Did the family anticipate my coming and decide to go to Walmart?

I began making other plans. "John, there is a young girl who will graduate from high school next week. I've had her on my heart. Let's drive by her house and see if it's a convenient time to study."

Her house was at the end of a dead-end street. When I turned into the driveway, I saw the father's car behind the house, so I backed out into the street and started away.

John asked, "Are you not going to stay?"

"No. Her dad is here. He hates the church and feels pretty much the same way about me. We can come back later." Suddenly a light turned on in my brain. I did a U-turn and drove right back into the driveway. The father was not at home. Within ten minutes, that young lady, accompanied by her mother, was on her way to be baptized into Christ.

Here is a question I had to ask myself: *Why did you back out of that driveway, Billy?* I will tell you the reason. I did not love that young girl or her soul as much as I should have. Otherwise, all the demons in hell could not have kept me out of that house. We need to learn to love the souls of people. We need to get back into the business of saving souls.

4. *Revival will sweeten our attitudes.* Do you know what happens when our attitudes are sweetened? All of the harsh, critical, fault-finding, judgmental attitudes disappear. When our attitude is sweetened, the brotherhood watchdogs and vigilantes disappear. As we pray for this revival and our attitude improves, do you know what will happen to our great brotherhood? We will no longer be fragmented. We will unite under the banner of Jesus Christ.

If only we could learn to love one another. In John 13:34–35, Jesus said,

> A new commandment I give to you, that you love one another; as I have loved you, that you also love one another. By this all will know that you are My disciples, if you have love for one another.

How do people know we're Christians? You may be thinking, "Well, Brother Lambert, we don't have mechanical musical instruments here." I was not asking how we worship.

How do they know we are Christians? You may also be thinking, "Well, Brother Lambert, it is because we baptize people for the remission of sins." I did not ask you how you become a Christian. I asked, "How do they know we are Christians?" It is certainly not because we have

"Church of Christ" in front of our building. Then why? It is the way we love and the attitude we have toward one another. A revival will sweeten our attitude.

5. *Revival will make us more spiritual and cause us to focus more on Jesus.* Paul said, "For to me, to live is Christ" (Philippians 1:21). Heaven is going to mean a great deal more to us now.

> If then you were raised with Christ, seek those things which are above, where Christ is, sitting at the right hand of God. Set your mind on things above, not on things on the earth (Colossians 3:1–2).

Our prayer for a revival of spirituality will cause us to dig deeply into the word of God. We will "search the Scriptures daily" (Acts 17:11) and "speak as the oracles of God" (1 Peter 4:11).

6. *Revival will help us save our homes.* Are you a Dr. Phil fan? Many of you see him on television, and we know about the epidemic in America that is worse than the West Nile virus. This epidemic is destroying families. According to Dr. Phil, fifty-seven percent of marriages now end in divorce.

It is time that we spread our hands out to God and pray, "Oh, please God, please give us a revival in these days. Help us save our homes and our families." Revival in the church begins with revival in the home, because the church will never be any stronger than the families that make it up.

- Pray that God will help us to be the right kind of fathers and husbands.
- Pray that God will help us to be the right kind of wives and mothers.
- Pray that God will help us be the right kind of sons or daughters.

We need to be praying, "Please God, please give us a little reviving."

Conclusion

Let's get right with God. The Fifty-first Psalm is a psalm of revival.

1. *David prayed that God would recognize the contrition of his heart.* "Have mercy upon me, O God, according to Your lovingkindness" (v. 1).
2. *David was willing to confess his sin to God.* "Against You, You only, have I sinned, and done this evil in your sight" (v. 4).
3. *David wanted God to cleanse him.* In verse 10, he continues, "Create in me a new heart, O God, and renew a steadfast spirit within me." David knew what it was to be in fellowship with God and in companionship and communion with God when he wrote Psalm 23. "The Lord is my shepherd, I shall not want." David wanted that same communion and fellowship when he said, "Do not cast me away from Your presence" (Psalm 51:11), and then in verse 12, "Restore to me the joy of Your salvation." He continues in verse 13, "Then I will teach transgressors Your ways; and sinners shall be converted to You."

Brethren, we will never have a revival in the Lord's church until we ourselves get right with God. We want to save our friends and our neighbors, but let us first be sure we are right with God. And let us pray, "Dear God, please God, give us a little reviving."

5

Twelve Hours to Live

In Luke 12:15 Jesus said, "Take heed and beware of covetousness, for one's life does not consist in the abundance of the things he possesses." He continues with the parable in verses 16–21,

> Then He spoke a parable to them, saying: The ground of a certain rich man yielded plentifully. And he thought within himself, saying, "What shall I do, since I have no room to store my crops?" So he said, "I will do this: I will pull down my barns and build greater, and there I will store all my crops and my goods. And I will say to my soul, 'Soul, you have many good laid up for many years; take your ease, eat, drink, and be merry.'" But God said to him, "Fool! This night your soul will be required of you; then whose will those things be which you have provided?" So is he who lays up treasure for himself, and is not rich toward God.

God Is Left Out

It will not be long until all of us are going to be on the other side of life's great divide. This is just a fact of life. Our text tells us about a man who met God in death. In life he had made some terrible blunders. His greatest mistake was that he left God out of his life. He talked about *my* goods and *my* fruits and *my* soul and *my* barns. But not one time did he give God any credit. A lot of people in America today are traveling down that very same path. They are leaving God out of their lives.

Another great blunder the man made was leaving other people out of his life. He referred to *his* goods. He was going to pull down *his* barns and build greater barns for all of *his* produce. He could not see a young woman who had just lost her means of income weeping beside the grave of her childhood sweetheart. He did not see hungry children who could have been helped without a great sacrifice on his part. He was thinking about himself and himself only.

Another mistake he made was assuming that he had a perpetual lease on life. His business mind assured him that he had plenty of goods laid up for many years. He thought he was going to live longer than he actually did. Most of us are going to die sooner than we think.

This man thought he could satisfy his soul with things stored in a barn, such as corn and hay. But he learned, as all men are going to learn, that he would never satisfy his soul's needs with things stored in a barn. Material things could never satisfy him.

So the man made a lot of mistakes. He was faced with the ultimate finality—his death. "This night, your soul will be required of you." Most of us are going to leave this world unexpectedly and probably with great suddenness.

A preacher friend of mine was driving the church bus one Sunday morning. He, his wife, and their children were on a familiar route to encourage children who would otherwise have no religious training. For some unknown reason—we will never know why—he drove the bus into the path of a train. He, his wife, and some of their children, along with several others, died that day. It never occurred to him on Saturday night when he was putting the final touches on his sermon that he had already preached his last sermon.

What Would You Want to Know?

God told the man in our text he would die that night. When I read this story, I always think, "What would I want to know if I just had twelve hours to live?"

1. *I would want to know that I was saved.* On a day-to-day basis, I want to know beyond any shadow of a doubt I am saved. Too many Christians when asked if they are saved, respond, "I think so. I hope so." However, we should know we are saved. Some have reason to believe they

might not be saved. Some have unreal expectations about what it means to live a Christian life. If you believe "I have to live it before I become a Christian," or "As a Christian, I can never make a mistake," then you have an unrealistic expectation of what it means to be a Christian.

- *Sometimes Christians are still in love with the world.* Christians are not perfect people; they are forgiven people. If we could live perfectly, we would not need the blood of Christ. But if we walk in the light as He is in the light and have fellowship one with another, then the blood of Christ cleanses us; that is, it continually cleanses us of our sins (1 John 1:7). It may be that you have doubts as to whether or not you are saved because you have never fallen out of love with the world (1 John 2:15–17).

  > A young boy is madly in love with a young girl. One day she tells him, "I don't want to have anything more to do with you." His heart is broken. He wonders, "What am I going to do?" But soon he falls in love with someone else.

  The reason many have doubts about salvation is because they are still in love with the world.
  Jesus said,

  > No one can serve two masters; for either he will hate the one and love the other, or else he will be loyal to the one and despise the other. You cannot serve God and mammon (Matthew 6:24).

  All of us know we cannot serve the devil and God at the same time. We cannot serve the world and God at the same time. Some of us try to live in the twilight zone, a place between those two extremes. If you are trying to do that, the doubts in your mind might be real.

- *A Christian may have doubts because he is neglecting Christian duties.* The Bible says that he who knows to do good and doesn't do it is sinning (James 4:17). So if you have been negligent, you may have real doubts about your salvation and your standing with God.

Many have said to me, "Billy, I don't believe a person can be certain about his salvation." Let me ask you a question. Are you really sure about that? I had a friend who had a sermon entitled, "It Is Good to Know and It Is Good to Know You Know." He developed the sermon on the basis of a blind man's statement: "One thing I know: that though I was blind, now I see" (John 9:25). I agree with his statement. It is good to know and it is good to know that you know.

Can you know anything? In Romans 2:2 the Bible says, "But we know that the judgment of God is according to truth." In Acts 2:36 Peter told the people on the day of Pentecost: "Let all the house of Israel know assuredly that God hath made this Jesus, whom you crucified, both Lord and Christ." If we can be sure that the judgment will be according to truth and we can be sure that Jesus is the Christ, then why can't we be sure we are saved?

You may be thinking, "I just don't know about that." Well, let us look at 2 Peter 1:10. "Therefore, brethren, be even more diligent to make your call and election sure." Peter says you can make it sure. In 2 Corinthians 5:1 Paul says, "For we know that if our earthly house, this tent, is destroyed, we have a building from God, a house not made with hands, eternal in the heavens."

Paul was not speculating, was he? He said, "For we *know.*" This is something we know. Look at 2 Timothy 1:12. "For I know whom I have believed and am persuaded that He is able to keep what I have committed to Him until that Day." Paul said, "I know." Hebrews 10:22 says, "Let us draw near with a true heart in full assurance of faith." So, we can be fully assured of our faith.

Turn to 1 John 2:3. "Now by this we know that we know Him." How will you know that you know that you know? How can you know Him? How can you be certain about your salvation? Read the rest of the verse: "Now by this we know that we know Him, *if we keep His commandments.*" And 1 John 5:13 says, "These things I have written to you who believe in the name of the Son of

God, that you may know that you have eternal life." John says you can know. Do you know you are saved?

If you only had a short time to live, you would want to know that, would you not? I would. I would want to be sure. I would want to know that I was saved.

- *Doubts may surface from a lack of Bible study.* You cannot know whether or not you are saved unless you study the Bible. That is why 2 Timothy 2:15 says, "Study to shew thyself approved unto God, a workman that needeth not to be ashamed, rightly dividing the word of truth" (KJV). We are to study the Bible to know what God wants us to do to be saved.

- *A lack of faith can cause a Christian to doubt his salvation.* But it is not enough to just study the Bible. We have to believe it. "Without faith it is impossible to please Him" (Hebrews 11:6). We must believe in Jesus. In John 8:24 Jesus said, "For if you do not believe that I am He, you will die in your sins." So we must believe in what we study in the Bible. In fact, the Bible is the source of our faith. Romans 10:17 says, "So then faith comes by hearing, and hearing by the word of God."

  I have a book in which the author states that faith is a miracle. Faith is not a miracle. Faith is a result of a teaching process. It is a result of having been taught the Bible. You cannot be saved unless you study the Bible and believe. You must believe in God and Jesus. You must believe that Christ is the Son of God.

  The only thing I have a right to ask anybody is, "Do you believe that Jesus Christ is the Son of God?"

- *Can you be sure of your salvation if you do not repent of your sins?* Listen to Jesus in Luke 13:3. "I tell you, no; but unless you repent you will all likewise perish." So it is repent or perish. It is turn or burn. Jesus said you must be willing to turn away from your sins. I cannot be sure I am saved unless I am a penitent believer.

- *If you have not confessed Jesus, you should doubt your salvation.* In Acts 8 a man asked a preacher this question, "Here is water. What hinders me from being baptized?" The preacher said, "If you believe with all your heart you may." The man responded, "I believe that Jesus Christ is the Son of God." You may wonder why we do this. Why would we want to confess the name of Jesus Christ in order to be saved? In Matthew 10:32–33 Jesus said,

> Therefore whoever confesses Me before men, him I will also confess also before My Father who is in heaven. But whoever denies Me before men, him I will also deny before My Father who is in heaven.

Confessing Christ is not something you do only one time. We confess Christ as the Son of God when we partake of the Lord's supper. We confess Christ as the Son of God in the songs we sing and the lives we lead. But as a believer ready to be saved, we must be willing to stand before others and say, "Jesus the Christ is the Son of the living God!" You cannot be sure you are saved unless you have done that.

• *You cannot be sure you are saved until you are scripturally baptized.* Scriptural baptism is a burial in water. Colossians 2:12 reads, "Buried with Him in baptism, in which you also were raised with Him through faith in the working of God, who raised Him from the dead." Scriptural baptism is indeed a burial in water. It must not be only that, but it must also be for the right reason and purpose. Jesus said, "He who believes and is baptized will be saved; but he who does not believe will be condemned" (Mark 16:16). So there are two conditions of salvation in this passage: belief and baptism. There is only one condition of condemnation: unbelief. It would have been redundant for Jesus to have said, "He that believeth not and is not baptized shall be condemned," because condemnation is a result of unbelief (John 3:18).

There are two conditions of salvation. Would you understand it if it read, "He that believes and is baptized shall receive a hundred dollar bill"? In order to receive the money, you believe and are baptized. But we are talking about something far greater than money—our soul's salvation. Jesus said, "He who believes and is baptized will be saved." You cannot be sure you are saved until you are scripturally baptized.

- *You cannot be sure that you are saved unless you are faithful to Christ.* Are you faithful? Are you really faithful? If someone asked you to write down on a 3 x 5 card whether or not you were saved, what would you write down? Yes, no, or a question mark? You have to leave the question mark out of it. The answer is yes or no—period.

2. *I would want to know that I was "right with other people."* We do not always know when we have offended others by our speech or actions. But when we know, we must make it right. You cannot live wrong and die right. We need to right the wrongs in our lives. Matthew 5:23–24 reads, "Therefore if you bring your gift to the altar, and there remember that your brother has something against you, leave your gift there before the altar, and go your way. First be reconciled to your brother, and then come and offer your gift."

Today we need people who can get along with others—folks like Abraham. He knew the fine art of getting along with others. As far as I know, he never took a Dale Carnegie course, but he knew how to win friends and influence people. Genesis 13 records a story about Abram, his nephew Lot, and their herdsmen. Confusion arose between the herdsmen. Listen to Abraham in verse 8: "Let there be no strife between you and me, between my herdsmen and your herdsmen." Well, why not, Uncle Abraham? The answer is simple: Because we are family; we are brethren, and we are to get along (Genesis 13:8).

We need brotherly love in the church. Hebrews 13:1 says, "Let brotherly love continue." Our love for one other should never cease. First Corinthians 13 says, "Love suffers long and is kind; love does not envy; love does not parade itself, is not puffed up; does not behave rudely, does not seek its own, is not provoked" (vv. 4–5). Are you easily provoked? The verse continues: "Thinks no evil; does not rejoice in iniquity, but rejoices in the truth; bears all things, believes all things, hopes all things, endures all things" (vv. 5–7). If I knew my days were numbered, I would want to be sure that I was right with other people.

3. *I would want to know that I was leaving a good influence behind me.* Every person reading this has an influence on others. We are creatures of influence. That may or may not be good, but it's true anyway. Because of our influence, we will be either stairs to heaven or stumbling blocks to eternal damnation. In Matthew 5:13 Jesus said, "You are the salt of the earth." We are to be a preserving influence on the world. He continues in verse 16: "Let your light so shine before men, that they many see your good works, and glorify your Father in heaven." We are to be lights in a dark world pillaged by sin.

In Matthew 13:33 Jesus said, "The kingdom of heaven is like leaven, which a woman took and hid in three measures of meal." Leaven influences a lump of meal. We are to have a leavening influence on this world.

On a little girl's tombstone were these words, "It was easier to be good when she was with us." Wouldn't that be a wonderful epitaph for your tombstone?

Most of you who hear me preach know I grew up in the sticks; at least, that is what we called it. We were Tennessee country people. Dad built our house with his own hands and it is still standing. We had indoor plumbing and a heating system called a fireplace. I am not sure the house was insulated. I remember getting up on those cold mornings and making a beeline to the fireplace, and then rotating like a roast on a rotisserie to get warm on all sides.

I know where we got the wood for the fireplace. We went to the locust tree forest on the back of our farm. We cut the trees, tied a log chain around them, and then Beth and ol' Matt dragged them back to the house. Dad cut the largest trees. They came crashing down with outstretched limbs, breaking limbs from smaller trees and smashing little saplings below. And so it is with our influence. When it falls short, we not only hurt ourselves but also the other trees (fellow Christians) and little saplings (children) around us. Those young in the faith are watching us. We are going to bring them down with us! I don't want to do that; I want to know that I have a good influence!

Here is an appropriate poem,

> I would rather see a sermon
> than to hear one any day.
> I'd rather one walk with me
> than merely tell the way.
> The eye's a better pupil
> and more willing than the ear.
> Fine counsel is confusing
> but example is always clear.
> —Selected

I want to know that I am leaving a good influence behind.

4. *I would want to know that I had won a soul for Christ.* Proverbs 11:30 says, "He who wins souls is wise." It takes wisdom to win souls. We ought to care about them. David was running away from Saul in Psalm 142:4 when he wrote, "No one cares for my soul." Can you imagine how he felt? God had only one Son. That Son was a champion winner of souls.

Why be concerned about the souls of others? God is concerned. "For God so loved the world that He gave His only begotten Son" (John 3:16). Jesus is concerned. "Greater love has no one than this, than to lay down one's life for his friends" (John 15:13). The Holy Spirit is concerned. "The Spirit and the bride say, 'Come!'" (Revelation 22:17). Heaven is concerned. In Luke 15 we are told there is joy in the presence of the angels of God over one sinner who repents. Even hell is concerned about souls. In Luke 16 there was a rich man, tormented in hell, who had five brothers. He wanted Lazarus to go back and preach to his brothers "lest they also come to this place of torment."

We too need to have concern. We need to care what happens to others. So if I had just a few short hours to live, I would want to know that I had won some souls. Maybe I had only invited them to come to a service or a meeting. Maybe all I had given them was a call. Maybe I had only mailed a brochure or prayed for them. But I had done something. I tried to win a soul to the Lord Jesus Christ.

Conclusion

We do not have long. I am made to realize this more as time passes. Our time is short and limited. I am not saying that to frighten you; I am saying that in order to get you to think.

If you had a short time to live, would you know that you are saved? Would you be right with others? Would you be leaving a good influence? Would you have done everything you could in order to influence others to go to heaven?

> A farmer needed a farm worker. He placed an ad in the newspaper offering food and lodging to a willing worker. The only person who applied for the job was a seventeen-year-old boy. The farmer would have liked someone more mature, but he had no choice but to hire him. A horrific storm arose the first night the young man was on the job. The farmer rushed into the boy's room. "Wake up! Wake up! He cried. We must go outside and get things secured! We have to get the cows in and cover up the hay! We have to get the machinery out of the weather!"
>
> The boy rolled over, opened one eye, and replied, "I can sleep when the wind blows." He rolled over and went back to sleep.
>
> In disgust the old farmer said, "I'll have to do it myself!" The farmer went out to the barn. The cows were in the barn, the hay was covered, and the machinery was in the shed. Only then did he understand the lad's words: "I can sleep when the wind blows." The new worker had everything taken care of! He had all his bases covered!

When the howling winds of eternity knock on your door, will you be able to enter a peaceful sleep? If you are saved, you will be. So get your heart right with God. Then you will know you can sleep when the wind blows.

6

Are You Prepared for Eternity?

"Therefore thus will I do to you, O Israel; because I will do this to you, prepare to meet your God, O Israel!" For behold, He who forms the mountains, and creates the wind, who declares to man what his thought is, and makes the morning darkness, who treads the high places of the earth—The Lord God of hosts is His name (Amos 4:12–13).

Israel had defied God. Now they are being called out into the open to face the issues that had been drawn up between them and God. One thing is very clear: A man should never select God as an opponent. We should never get ourselves on the wrong side of God. In our reading, Amos told us why.

- *God is not limited in power.* He formed the mountains and He created the winds. He is called "Almighty God."
- *He is not limited in knowledge.* He declares His thoughts to man. There is nothing about us that God does not know. He even knows your thoughts right now.
- *He is not limited by space.* He makes the morning darkness and He treads upon the high places of the earth. He is the God who is here, who is there, and who is everywhere.
- *God is the God of hosts, the God of battles.* Any individual makes a grave mistake when he selects God as his opponent.

How Men Meet God

Amos told Israel to prepare to meet their God. There are many ways men meet God.

1. *Nature.* The Bible says, "The heavens declare the glory of God; and the firmament shows His handiwork" (Psalm 19:1). We see God in the golden sunset, in the Milky Way, and in the stars that shine like diamonds. We hear the voice of God in the birds, in the murmur of the brook, and in the ebbing and flowing of the tides. We meet God in nature.

2. *Worship.* Jesus said, "Where two or three are gathered together in My name, I am there in the midst of them" (Matthew 18:20). The Lord is always with us when we worship in spirit.

3. *His revelation*—the revealed Word. We see design in the universe and are convinced there is a designer. That designer is God. The Bible plainly tells us so. It tells us there is one God who is above all, through all, and in you all.

4. *Death.* After that we are going to meet God in the judgment. "It is appointed for men to die once, but after this the judgment" (Hebrews 9:27). All of us are going to stand before Him and give an account of our lives. The Bible says in 2 Corinthians 5:10, "We must all appear before the judgment seat of Christ." There are no exceptions. All of us will one day appear before the judgment seat of Christ.

Great Days of Preparation

Think of all the great days in the history of the world:

- It was a great day when God formed man out of the dust of the ground. He breathed into his nostrils the breath of life and man became a living soul.
- It was a great day when God put the sun, the moon, and the stars in their places in the heavens.
- It was a great day when God came down on Mount Sinai and gave the Ten Commandments, the first written divine law, to the Hebrew people.
- It was a great day when the Lord Jesus Christ was born and the angels sang: "And on earth peace, goodwill toward men" (Luke 2:14).

- It was a great day when the Lord Jesus Christ died on the cross at Calvary for the sins of humanity.
- It was a great day when He was raised from the dead by the power of God.
- It will be a great day, a day from which all other days will be made, when we meet God in judgment.

Amos said "Prepare to meet your God" (Amos 4:12). We have to prepare for almost everything now. Preparation is essential in education. There are many would-be scholars who do not make the grade because they are not prepared. Preparation is essential in every worthwhile aspect of life. Consider medicine as an example. For an individual to become a competent, practicing physician, years of preparation and study are required. Preparation is essential in the realm of athletics. Coaches have long been aware that young men and women must have extensive training in order to compete on the athletic field. They need to have a winning attitude.

But there is no area of preparation more important than in spiritual matters. So prepare to meet thy God.

Why Prepare to Meet God?

Why should we prepare to meet God in eternity? Here are three reasons.

1. The command to do it makes it mandatory.
2. The attempt to overcome sin makes it obligatory.
3. The nature of heaven demands it.

Listen to Amos: "Prepare to meet your God." In Romans 14:12 Paul says, "So then each of us shall give account of himself to God." This is another way of saying we had better prepare to meet God. Some speak of essential and non-essential commands. I was not aware that God had non-essential commands. Every command God has given is an essential command. Even if there were no place other than Amos 4:12 in the entire Bible that teaches us to prepare to meet God, I would believe it, because God does not have to make a statement but one time to mean it. He does not have to say the same thing over and over again to mean it. When He says it one time, that is enough.

Commands: One Reason is Enough

I had a close friend, a minister of the gospel, who is now deceased. He once told me that he had a sermon entitled "32 Reasons Why You Need to Be Baptized." How would you like to sit through that one if he spent three minutes on each point? Your ninety-six minutes at his feet would seem like all day. I wanted to tell him that one reason is enough! That is because God said to do it. If there were no verse in the Bible that told Billy Lambert to be prepared to meet God except Amos 4:12, I would believe it. So why should I do it? Because God said to do it. You need to prepare.

Sin: Escape It!

Another reason we need to prepare to meet God is because of sin. We sometimes are tempted to act like the ostrich—we hide our heads in the sand rather than confront reality. Let me tell you what the Bible says about it in Hebrews 3:13: "But exhort one another daily, while it is called 'Today,' lest any of you be hardened through the deceitfulness of sin." I do not know of anything more deceitful than sin. Sin promises one thing and gives something else. It promises salvation and gives damnation. It promises light and gives darkness. It promises freedom and gives slavery. It is exceedingly deceitful! I need to prepare to meet God because of the sin in my life.

Heaven: Don't Miss It

I need to prepare to meet God because the nature of heaven demands it. What kind of place is heaven, anyway? It is a prepared place. The Lord said, "I go and prepare a place for you. And if I go and prepare a place for you, I will come again and receive you to Myself; that where I am, there you may be also" (John 14:2–3). In Matthew 25:34 we read, "Then the King will say to those on his right hand, 'Come, you blessed of my Father, inherit the kingdom prepared for you from the foundation of the world.'" This is a prepared place for prepared people. A prepared place for unprepared people is just not quite right. An unprepared place for prepared people is not right either.

But a prepared place for people who are prepared is exactly right. So I need to prepare to meet God.

How to Prepare to Meet God

How do we go about doing that? I am not trying to play with your mind. This is too serious. Think with me logically. If we could learn what people in Bible times did to prepare and we could do that today, why could we not be prepared to meet God? Is that not logical? If we find out what they did and do what they did, we would be prepared. Right?

- *Be taught and be baptized.* In Acts 2 we read of the beginning of the church. This chapter contains the first announcement of conditions of salvation under the worldwide commission. Our Lord had said, "Go therefore and make disciples of all nations" (Matthew 28:19). He said for them to be taught and baptized in the name of the Father, the Son, and the Holy Spirit. Acts 2 is a record of how people were taught to prepare to meet God.

- *Worship on Sunday.* Acts 2 begins with Pentecost, a Jewish holy day. "When the Day of Pentecost had fully come, they were all with one accord in one place" (v. 1). In the book of Leviticus, the Jewish people were told to count seven Sabbath days (49 days). Then on the day following the seventh Sabbath, they were to observe Pentecost. So Pentecost was always a first day of the week. So why do we worship on Sunday? The church began on that day. Who is the "they" in this verse? Look at Acts 1:26; the last noun is "apostles." The chapter divisions were added later to our English Bibles to aid us in our study. If there were no chapter division, it would be obvious that "they" refers to the apostles.

Miracle Matters

And suddenly there came a sound from heaven, as of a rushing mighty wind, and it filled the whole house where they were sitting. And there appeared to them divided tongues, as of fire, and one sat upon each of them. And they were all filled with the Holy Spirit and began to speak with other tongues, as the Spirit gave them utterance (Acts 2:2–4).

Now look in verse 5. "And there were dwelling at Jerusalem Jews, devout men, from every nation under heaven." These were devout men, not cranks or crackpots. They were devout men.

And when this sound occurred, the multitude came together, and were confused, because everyone heard them speak in his own language. Then they were all amazed and marveled, saying to one another, "Look, are not all these who speak Galileans? And how is it that we hear, each in our own language in which we were born? Parthians and Medes and Elamites, those dwelling in Mesopotamia, Judea and Cappadocia, Pontus and Asia, Phrygia and Pamphylia, Egypt and the parts of Libya adjoining Cyrene, visitors from Rome, both Jews and proselytes, Cretans and Arabs—we hear them speaking in our own tongues the wonderful works of God (Acts 2:6–11).

The apostles were speaking in tongues. Was that some type of ecstatic utterance? Was it some type of gibberish that could not be understood? No, when they spoke in tongues they were speaking in languages other people could understand. There was a miracle. The apostles were baptized with the Holy Spirit on the day of Pentecost and received the gift of being able to speak in languages they had not studied! Why this gift? They were given these so those gathered there could understand their preaching. The audience heard them speak in their dialects. They heard their native languages.

Some may think that the miracle occurred on the ears of the hearers rather than the tongues of the speakers. No. Some may think that the miracle must have occurred sometime between the time the apostles spoke and the time the people heard it. No. Here is the miracle: God endowed the apostles with the power and ability to speak in foreign languages so that they could preach to the people who spoke different languages.

All Shook Up by Prophecy

This event shook everyone up. So in verse 12 they ask the question, "Whatever could this mean?" Some mocked, accusing them of being drunk: "They are full of new wine." But Peter, one of the eleven, stood up and said, "These are not drunk, as you suppose, since it is only the third hour of the day. But this is what was spoken by the prophet Joel" (Acts 2:14–16). They were seeing the fulfillment of prophesy in Joel 2:28–32. It was being fulfilled. Then Peter quotes Joel's prophesy. "It shall come to pass in the last days" (Acts 2:17).

Have you ever heard a preacher talk about the "last days" as if it just happened? How long have we been in the last days? We have been in the last days since Pentecost. We are in the last days. We are in the last age of Bible history. There will not be one after this. So Joel's prophesy was,

> And it shall come to pass in the last days, says God, that I will pour out My Spirit on all flesh; your sons and your daughters shall prophesy, your young men shall see visions, your old men shall dream dreams. And also on My menservants and on My maidservants I will pour out My Spirit in those days; and they shall prophesy. I will show wonders in the heavens and in the earth: blood and fire and pillars of smoke. The sun shall be turned into darkness, and the moon into blood, before the coming of the great and awesome day of the Lord. And it shall come to pass that whoever calls on the name of the Lord shall be saved (Acts 2:17–21; cf. Joel 2:28–32).

This is what Peter said in verse 22:

> Men of Israel, hear these words: Jesus of Nazareth, a Man attested by God to you by miracles, wonders, and signs which God did through Him in your midst, as you yourselves also know—Him, being delivered by the determined purpose and foreknowledge of God, you have taken by lawless hands, have crucified, and put to death; whom God raised up, having loosed the pains of death, because it was not possible that He should be held by it (Acts 2:22–24).

Who is he talking about? Jesus. He said I want you to know that the one that was crucified, was a man approved of God and by the wonders and signs, which He did.

Why They Listened

Notice the phrase, "As you yourselves also know" (Acts 2:22). They did not deny that he was telling the truth. They could not and did not. I have often thought that if there were ever a group of people that could refute the resurrection of Jesus, it was these people. They could not disprove it because they knew Peter was telling the truth. Peter also told them that they were guilty for the death of Christ, just as we are. Our sins put Him on the cross. Peter continues that He was raised from the dead by the power of God. They may have just "blown that off," as some young people say.

However, if there was one person that they would pay attention to it was their prophet David. Peter continues,

> For David says concerning Him: "I foresaw the Lord always before my face, for He is at my right hand, that I may not be shaken. Therefore my heart rejoiced, and my tongue was glad; moreover my flesh also will rest in hope. For You will not leave my soul in Hades, nor will You allow Your Holy One to see corruption" (Acts 2:25–27).

Peter is now quoting what David said in the Psalm 16. Briefly notice what Peter says about Jesus in his inspired commentary on Psalm 16. "He, foreseeing this, spoke concerning the resurrection of the Christ, that His soul was not left in Hades, nor did His flesh see corruption" (Acts 2:31). Peter observes that when David talked about that, he was talking about the resurrected Christ: "This Jesus God has raised up" (Acts 2:32).

The Crowd's Response

He continues in verse 36 as he draws his sermon to a conclusion,

> Therefore let all the house of Israel know assuredly that God has made this Jesus, whom you crucified, both Lord and Christ. Now when they heard this, they were cut to the heart, and said to Peter and the rest of the apostles, "Men and brethren, what shall we do?"

Peter was preaching Jesus to them. When they learned that it was Jesus who was crucified and died, they were pricked in their hearts. Then thousands asked "What shall we do?"

My Response

You may be asking, "What do I need to do? What do I need to do to get right with God? What do I do?" Those men also asked this question. Notice in verse 38 the answer they were given. This may not be what you have heard other preachers say. I do not want to know what other preachers have said. I want to hear what God has to say. This is what Peter said to do to prepare to meet God: "Repent." If there ever was a time in the world when people needed to repent, surely it was the people who crucified Jesus. Before we begin being censoring people, let me remind you that our sins also put Him on the cross. We need to repent, too.

Is there anything else we need to do Peter? He continues, "and be baptized." The word *baptism* literally means to be immersed or plunged. This word is not a translation; rather, it is transliterated. It carries from the Greek language into the English language. It would translate "Repent and be immersed" or "Repent and be buried in water."

How many of us ought to do that, Peter? "Every one of you," he says. Is that still true today? Yes, everyone needs to do that. By whose authority should we do that? Peter continues, "in the name of Jesus Christ." It is also in the authority of Christ in Matthew 28:19 that we baptize in the name of the Father, the Son, and the Holy Spirit. Why should we repent and be baptized? Peter continues, "for the remission of sins." What are we going to get out of it, Peter? "And you shall receive the gift of the Holy Spirit." The Holy Spirit is not the donor; He is the donation.

Here is the answer to their question, "What shall we do?" They were told to repent of their sins and be baptized. Remember, our Lord said, "He who believes and is baptized will be saved" (Mark 16:16). Peter said, "Repent, and let every one of you be baptized."

Did they do this? Look in verse 41. "Then," which is the same day, Pentecost, the first day of the week, "those who gladly received his word were baptized: and that day about three thousand souls were added unto them." Have you ever been to a service like that? I haven't. There were three thousand people baptized for the remission of their sins that day.

Baptized Believers Added to the Church

I wonder what church they joined. Look in verse 47. "Praising God and having favor with all the people. And the Lord added to the church daily those who were being saved." Jesus had said, "I will build My church" (Matthew 16:18). When people believed in Jesus, repented of their sins, and as penitent, confessing believers were baptized for the remission of their sins, they were added to the church. In Bible times they were just added to the church of the Lord. That was all. They were part of the church, the church that Jesus said He would build.

Your Destiny

We wanted to find out what people did in Bible times to prepare to meet God. If you have not done it, the time to prepare is now. Tomorrow you could be so hardened against the message that it might not appeal to you. Tomorrow you could be dead. Tomorrow the Lord could come. Tomorrow we could be in judgment. Tomorrow could be too late. Now is the only time you have. Do you need to make some spiritual preparation? This is your eternal destiny. Are you prepared for eternity?

7

Five Minutes After I Die

An Appointment to Keep

In Job 14:14, Job asked, "If a man dies, shall he live again?" Few subjects interest men more than the subject of life after death. There may be a number of reasons for our curiosity about this subject. One of the reasons is that we have never experienced death, and mystery always surrounds the unknown.

Another reason we are curious about life after death is the certainty of our own death. Every time I am called to the side of a grieving family, I wonder who's going to be next, because this I know: "It is appointed for men to die once" (Hebrews 9:27). None of us can do anything about that. We can exercise, sleep right, eat right, take our vitamins, and take all kinds of precautions, but the edict has gone forth: *It is appointed for man to die once.*

Human wisdom cannot outsmart death or else Solomon, the world's wisest man, would not have died. Human strength cannot avail against the warrior called death or else Samson would not have died. Righteousness cannot withstand its onslaught or else Peter, Paul, James, John, and a host of other righteous people would not have died. No, man cannot outlive his liability or else Methuselah, the world's oldest man, would not have died. *It is appointed for man to die once.*

I Will Be Alive

I suppose the clearest teaching in the Bible about the state of the dead is that of the rich man and Lazarus:

There was a certain rich man who was clothed in purple and fine linen and fared sumptuously every day. But there was a certain beggar named Lazarus, full of sores, who was laid at his gate, desiring to be fed with the crumbs which fell from the rich man's table. Moreover the dogs came and licked his sores. So it was that the beggar died, and was carried by the angels to Abraham's bosom. The rich man also died and was buried. And being in torments in Hades, he lifted up his eyes and saw Abraham afar off, and Lazarus in his bosom. Then he cried and said, "Father Abraham, have mercy on me, and send Lazarus that he may dip the tip of his finger in water and cool my tongue, for I am tormented in this flame." But Abraham said, "Son, remember that in your lifetime you received your good things, and likewise Lazarus evil things; but now he is comforted and you are tormented. And besides all this, between us and you there is a great gulf fixed, so that those who want to pass from here to you cannot, nor can those from there pass to us." Then he said, "I beg you therefore, father, that you would send him to my father's house, for I have five brothers, that he may testify to them, lest they also come to this place of torment." Abraham said to him, "They have Moses and the prophets; let them hear them." And he said, "No, father Abraham, but if one goes to them from the dead, they will repent." But he said to him, "If they do not hear Moses and the prophets, neither will they be persuaded though one rise from the dead" (Luke 16:19–31).

We learn from that reading what will be true immediately after death. Five minutes after I die, I will be alive. You see, the rich man was still alive; Lazarus was still alive; Abraham was still alive. Man is a composite being—body and spirit.

In 2 Corinthians 4:16 Paul said, "Therefore we do not lose heart. Even though our outward man is perishing, yet the inward man is being renewed day by day." There is an outward man. That is what you can see of me. But everyone has an inward man you do not see, and when a man dies, his inward man separates from his outward man.

James 2:26 says, "For as the body without the spirit is dead, so faith without works is dead also." So when an individual dies, the spirit goes into the care and keeping of God and the body is deposited in the earth. There is the departure of man's spirit, man's soul, from the body.

Rachel

The Bible describes Rachel's dying moments with these words: "As her soul was departing . . ." (Genesis 35:18). Her soul left her body—she died. When it leaves the body, the soul continues to live. For example, in Revelation 6:9 John said, "I saw under the altar the souls of those who had been slain for the word of God and for the testimony which they held." What did John see? He saw the souls of martyred saints. He saw those who had given their lives for the cause of Christ. They were dead in that their souls had been separated from their bodies, but their souls continued to live. Man's soul continues to exist.

Prophets on the Mount

In Matthew 17 Jesus Christ took Peter, James, and John to a high mountain by themselves, and there He was transfigured before them. Upon that mountain there appeared with them Moses and Elijah. Moses was the lawgiver; Elijah was the dean of the prophets. And so, as it were, the law and the prophets came to lay down their authority at the feet of Jesus. On that occasion, God said, "This is My beloved Son, in whom I am well pleased. Hear Him!" (Matthew 17:5). Here were men who had been dead for hundreds of years, and yet were still alive and speaking with the Lord. You see, five minutes after I die, I will be alive.

I Will Have My Memory

Five minutes after I die, I will still have my memory. I'm thankful for that because there are days that I don't have it too good in this life. Abraham said, "Son, remember . . ." He was saying, *I want you to remember Lazarus. I want you to remember how bad he had it. I want you to remember how good you had it. Son, remember.*

Have you ever thought what a blessing it is to be able to remember? If you did not have the ability to remember, you wouldn't know who you are right now. You would not know where you are or why you're here. If you didn't have the ability to remember, you wouldn't know where to go in the next ten minutes. It is a great blessing to be able to remember.

> A young boy preacher was going to conduct his first wedding ceremony. He went to an older preacher for advice. The older preacher said, "Memorize it, son. It will just be a lot more impressive and effective if you do not get up and read everything." The young man said, "Well, suppose I forget something?" The older consoled, "Just pick out a scripture you know and quote it. Nobody will know the difference. They'll think it's a part of the ceremony. That will give you time to think about what else you want to say, and then you can go on."
>
> On the day of the wedding, the young preacher started very well—for about five minutes. Then his mind went blank. He couldn't think of anything he had memorized, but he did remember to quote a scripture. But in that tense moment, he could remember only one: "Father, forgive them, for they know not what they do" (Luke 23:34).

Memory is a great blessing. And it is sad to see people lose their ability to remember. A policeman from the city of Mobile called one day asking if I knew a certain lady.

"Yes, I know Gladys," I replied.

"Well," he responded, "we found her wandering on the streets, and the only thing she could remember was Central Church of Christ."

Shortly a police car drove up in front of my office. The lady in question was a pitiful sight. She had on two dresses—both turned backwards and wrong side out. She didn't know who I was. She didn't even know where she belonged. And to tell you the truth, I didn't either, because she had moved recently. After several phone calls we finally figured out where to direct her and the policeman.

It is sad when people lose their memory, but I know one thing. Five minutes after I die, I'll have my memory. And so will you. We're going to remember neglected opportunities. We're going to remember sermons we've heard. We're going to remember unread Bibles in our homes. We're going to remember prayers we have prayed—or maybe those we should have prayed. We're going to remember wrongs we didn't make right. And we're going to remember the great love of God. You're going to have a long, long time to think about it. Yes, we will have our memory.

I Will Learn That God Means What He Says

Five minutes after I die, I will learn that God meant what He said. The rich man learned that lesson the hard way, didn't he? Some today seem to think God doesn't mean what He says. They say, "I know that's in the Bible, I know God said that, but it's okay not to do it."

- *Titus 1:2.* "In hope of eternal life which God, that cannot lie, promised before time began." God tells the truth, friends.
- *2 Peter 3:9.* "The Lord is not slack concerning His promise." God means what He says.
- *Romans 3:4.* "Let God be true but every man a liar." God has meant what He said in every age.

In the Beginning

Back in Genesis 2 God put Adam and Eve in the Garden of Eden. They were to dress and to keep the garden. Their only prohibition was not to eat of the fruit of the tree in the midst of the garden. God said in Genesis 2:17, "The day that you eat of it you shall surely die." We know the rest of the story, don't we? We know that they ate of that forbidden fruit. And as a result, sin entered into the world, and death by sin. Six thousand years of thorns and thistles and crying and sighing and dying tell us that God meant what he said to Adam in the very beginning.

In the Mosaical Age

God meant what He said in the Mosaical Age. In Leviticus 10 we read about two priests whose names are Nadab and Abihu. They were sons of Aaron. They got it in their minds that they could worship as they wanted to, without regard to God's instructions, so they offered "strange fire" on the altar. As a result of offering fire that God had neither specified nor sanctified, God took their lives. Some people today would have reasoned like this: "One fire is as good as another fire." But one fire wasn't as good as another fire, because God told them what He wanted, and He meant what He said.

In This Age

And God means what he says in this age of the world—in the Christian Age. In Hebrews 12:25, the Bible says,

> See that you do not refuse Him who speaks. For if they did not escape who refused Him who spoke on earth, much more shall not we escape if we turn away from Him who speaks from heaven.

That's another way of saying we have to be careful how we conduct ourselves because God Almighty means what He says.

He means what He says about sin, that the wages of sin is death. He means what He says about salvation, that salvation is in Christ and only in Him. In 2 Timothy 2:10 Paul wrote, "I endure all things for the sake of the elect, that they also may obtain the salvation which is in Christ Jesus with eternal glory."

God means what He says about the location of salvation. It is not found outside of Christ. Salvation is found only in the Lord Jesus Christ! That's where all spiritual blessings are. Look in Ephesians 1:3. "Blessed be the God and Father of our Lord Jesus Christ, who has blessed us with every spiritual blessing in the heavenly places in Christ." All spiritual blessings are in Christ. The only place you can be a new creature is in Jesus. In 2 Corinthians 5:17 we read, "If any one is in Christ, he is a new creation: old things have passed away; behold, all things have become new." Salvation is in Christ. Spiritual blessings are in Christ. You become a new creature in the Lord Jesus Christ. So tell us, Paul, how to get into Jesus Christ. Find Paul's answer in Galatians 3:26–27 (KJV):

- *For ye are all the children of God* . . . That's what we want to be, isn't it? We all want to be children of God.

- *By faith,* that is, by the system of faith in contrast to the system of works in the Old Testament. Look at the context of Galatians 3, and you will that's what he means. So we are children of God by faith. Where?

- *In Christ Jesus.* We're children of God by faith in Christ. If that's the case, Paul, tell us how we get into Christ? Look at the very next verse.

- *For as many of you as have been*—Have been what?

- *Baptized into Christ have put on Christ.* Now that's pretty simple, isn't it, getting into Christ where there is salvation, where we have all spiritual blessings, and where we can be new creatures in Him? And I want to tell you something as kindly as I know how, and yet as frankly as I must. God means that. He means what He says about salvation.

A man asked his friend, "Do you think God meant what He said?" His friend replied, "Well, if He didn't mean what He said, I wish He'd said what He meant." I rather think God meant what He said, don't you? And five minutes after I die, I will know that—that He meant what He said.

The Door of Opportunity Will Be Closed

Five minutes after I die, the door of opportunity will be closed. It was closed for that rich man. The first thing he asked for was personal mercy. He said, "Father Abraham, have mercy on me" (Luke 16:24). Do you wonder what people in hell want today? They want mercy. He said, *Have mercy. Send Lazarus. All I want him to do is just take his finger, moisten the end of his finger and place that on my tongue. I'm tormented!* Abraham said, *Well, that's just not possible.* Time had run out for the rich man. All his opportunities were gone.

Right now is the only time you have to be the right kind of husband and father. Listen!—every husband and every father. Sometimes we get so caught up in making a living for our family that we forget to make a life for them. We forget that our family needs spiritual direction. Our wife and children need spiritual guidance. They need spiritual leadership. And, oh, that God would raise up more men today like Joshua, men who say, "As for me and my house, we will serve the Lord" (Joshua 24:15). Men, this is the only opportunity you have. One day that door of opportunity will be closed.

Ladies, now is the only opportunity you have to be the kind of wife and the kind of mother you ought to be. As a mother, you ought to be able to look into the faces of your children and tell them, "I want you to be just like me, because I'm trying to be like the Lord Jesus Christ. I'm trying to serve the Lord, and I want you to follow my example." One day that opportunity will be gone.

Now is the only opportunity you have to obey God. Someday the door will be closed. You have to obey God while your mind is normal and while you can understand the message. I've dealt with those who couldn't understand new concepts— who had reached the time in life when they couldn't be reached by the gospel. You have to obey God while the message appeals to you. I've seen people become so seared and so hardened to the gospel message that it didn't really appeal to them. In Ephesians 4:19 Paul talked about people who get past feeling.

To this day there is no paved road to the place where my brothers and I grew up. It is a long way out in the country. After a cold winter, we could hardly wait for the weather to warm enough for us to walk outside barefooted. At first those old rocks punctured our feet—they bled. But by the end of the summer, we could run up and down that graveled road without a problem. Fire almost flew from our feet. What happened? Our feet got tough; they hardened. Hardness can also happen to your heart.

Now is the only time you have. You need to come now while the message appeals to you. Don't become hardened and seared. Come while life lasts. Yes, five minutes after I die, the door of opportunity will be closed.

Queen Mary lay dying. Here she was a wealthy woman. Do you know what she said? "I'd give a thousand dollars for just a moment of time." But it was too late.

I'll Be Somewhere in Eternity

Five minutes after I die I'm going to be somewhere in eternity. That rich man is in eternity, isn't he? Eternity. It begins where human computation ends. Men can tell you about the stars, their distance from the earth and their size, but they can't tell you anything about eternity. Man can tell you about the weather. They can tell you the kind of weather we're going to have today, next week, next month, maybe the rest of this year. But they can't tell you anything about eternity.

Suppose the Pacific Ocean and the Atlantic Ocean were landlocked. Then suppose a tiny sparrow took a drop of water from the Pacific, flew across the United States, and deposited that drop into the Atlantic. Then suppose she repeats that process time and again until the Pacific Ocean is empty. The time involved would be nothing compared to eternity.

> When we've been there ten thousand years,
> Bright shining as the sun,
> We've no less days to sing God's praise
> Than when we've first begun.

The Christian can thank God for that!

Conclusion

We have been discussing a profound subject: "Five Minutes after I Die." In 1 Samuel 20:3 David said there's just "a step between me and death." That's a step you will take, and that's a step I will take. No one will ever be able to take that step for us. When Joab saw David's rebellious son suspended in a terebinth tree, he pierced his heart through with three spears. When David received the news, he was grieved: "O my son Absalom—my son, my son Absalom—if only I had died in your place! O Absalom my son, my son!" (2 Samuel 18:33). But he didn't, and he could not have, could he? And death's a step from which there is no return.

Another son of David died. As David wept over that infant, he said, "I shall go to him, but he shall not return to me" (2 Samuel 12:23). Death is a step between time and eternity, a step in which permanent changes are made. This is a step for which we need to prepare.

8

The World's Greatest Question

The Bible Is Full of Questions

"Where are you?" God asked that question in Genesis 3:9, not because He was unaware of Adam's whereabouts, but because He wanted Adam to know something of the mess he was in. *Where are you, Adam?* That's a good question for us to consider? Where are we in the sight of God?

"Am I my brother's keeper?" (Genesis 4:9). It would have been far better had Cain been his brother's keeper than his brother's murderer. Is there a sense in which each of us is our brother's keeper?

Job asks the question, "If a man dies, shall he live again?" (Job 14:14). When Christ came into the world, He answered that question for time and eternity by saying, "I am the resurrection and the life. He who believes in Me, though he may die, he shall live" (John 11:25).

In Matthew 16:26 Jesus asks, "For what profit is it to a man if he gains the whole world, and loses his own soul? Or what will a man give in exchange for his soul?" If we chose to have all this world offers at the expense of our own souls, we would have made a poor bargain indeed.

"How shall we escape if we neglect so great a salvation?" is the question in Hebrews 2:3. That really is one of those questions that answers itself because there is no escape when an individual neglects the salvation offered through the Lord Jesus Christ.

The Greatest Question

A number of great questions are found in the Bible, but there are none greater than the one that we find in Acts 16:30: "Sirs, what must I do to be saved?"

> Several years ago, I was in a meeting in Alabama. When I got to town, the preacher said, "There is a man in town who would like to have a religious debate with you this week." I said, "If he'll come to hear me preach, I'll talk to him."
>
> He showed up one night although I did not think it was to hear me preach. Nonetheless, I met with him for the great religious debate at the civic center in downtown Lafayette, Alabama. Back in those days, the "civic center" in Lafayette was the local Standard Oil Service Station. That was where the town gathered. So we sat down, and this man began to tell how long the earth was going to last. He said that kingdoms had not been established. He went on and on.
>
> After several minutes, I finally said, "I hear what you are saying, but really, what difference do those things make if we do not have the answer to the greatest question in all the Bible?"
>
> He said, "Well, what is that?"
>
> We turned to Acts 16:30 which I believe with all my heart is the world's greatest question: "Sirs, what must I do to be saved?"

"Must" Is Imperative

Analyze the question for a minute. The person asked, "What must I do?" He did not ask, "What *might* I do?" or "What *could* I do?" His question was far more imperative: "What *must* I do?" It was something like Jesus' statement in John 3:7: "You must be born again." Jesus did not say that it is a good idea or it is a suggestion for you to be born again. Rather, Jesus said, "You *must* be born again." So here is the question again: "What *must* I do to be saved?"

"I" Means "Me"

Also notice the "I" in the question, "What must *I* do to be saved?" This makes the question personal, does it not? He is not asking what did Abraham, Moses, or the thief on the cross had to do. Rather he is asking, "What must *I* do to be saved?" It is a personal question. The fact is Christianity is a personal religion. Jesus Christ died for you. Think about Paul's statement:

> I have been crucified with Christ; it is no longer I who live, but Christ lives in me; and the life which I now live in the flesh I live by faith in the Son of God, who loved me, and gave Himself for me (Galatians 2:20).

That is, He loved Paul and He gave Himself for Paul. You could put your name there. He loved me. He loved Billy. He loved Paul. He loved Leo, Lomax, and Wilmer. He loves us all. It is personal. It is, "What must *I* do?"

Do!

Notice the question again: "What must I *do?*" There is something on a man's part that he must do, and there is a divine side of salvation, such as the shed blood of Jesus Christ. This is God's part in our salvation. But there is something on a man's part that he must do in response to what God has done. So each person must ask, "What must I *do?*"

This question suggests man's inability to direct himself. Why else would he ask, "What must I do?" Too many people today want to tell you and God what they are doing to be saved. They want to give God directions. But man is incapable of devising a way to be saved. That reminds me of the prophecy of Jeremiah 10:23: "O Lord, I know the way of man is not in himself; it is not in man who walks to direct own steps." There is not a soul today who can successfully direct his life without God.

To Be Saved

And then notice the question again. "What must I do *to be saved?*" The opposite of saved is lost. I cannot think of a word in the English language that is more frightening than the word *lost*.

> I remember a number of years ago; I was in a meeting in northeast Mississippi. It was around 9:30 in the evening on the last day of the meeting and we were late because we had baptized several people. Brother Henry Harville and I were about to leave the parking lot when we heard sobs and screams coming from his son Archie's house. As we rushed toward the

front door, Archie's wife Rosa came running out and scream-
ing, "Brother Lambert, Brother Lambert, my baby is lost."
Archie was a shift worker and had been sleeping. The baby
had awakened and walked out of the house into the darkness.
A sinking feeling overwhelmed me. A frantic search ensued.
At last we found the little boy sitting on his daddy's tractor out
in the garden!

Think about miners trapped in man-made caverns far below earth's surface. The community and nation rejoices when
they are rescued—if they are. Imagine being trapped under-
ground in total darkness with food depleted and water running low, totally cut off from coworkers whom you know are
trying with all their might to rescue you.

Imagine being lost at sea, clinging to a raft or a scrap of
wood from a sunken vessel. Many survivors in their panic let
go of their only hope and slowly sink into the depths of the
vast ocean—lost.

But I will tell you something far worse than that—the loss
of your soul. The question is, "What must I do *to be saved*?"
What must I do to save my soul?

God Desires Man's Salvation

When we start to answer this question, we need divine
direction. What did God say? He "desires all men to be saved
and to come to the knowledge of the truth" (1 Timothy 2:4). No
one wants men to be saved more than God does.

> The Lord is not slack concerning His promise, as some count
> slackness, but is longsuffering toward us, not willing that any
> should perish but that all should come to repentance (2 Peter
> 3:9).

It is not the will, the decree, or the desire of God Almighty
that one single person is lost. It is God's desire that all people
be saved.

Have you ever wondered why people will be lost? Some
believe that a certain number of people are going to be saved
and no more, but the Bible gives a different reason: "Whoever
desires, let him take the water of life freely" (Revelation 22:17).
In Matthew 11:28 the Lord says, "Come to Me, all you who
labor and are heavy laden, and I will give you rest." All who

come to Christ can be saved. No one will be lost because all salvation reservations have been filled.

Men will not be lost because they cannot understand how to be saved. Jesus said, "And you shall know the truth, and the truth shall make you free" (John 8:32). He did not say you will have to speculate or wonder about the truth. He said you will know the truth. You can understand the truth and that the truth will set you free from sin.

> And an highway shall be there, and a way, and it shall be called The way of holiness; the unclean shall not pass over it . . . the wayfaring men, though fools, shall not err therein (Isaiah 35:8 KJV).

The highway of holiness that leads to heaven is so plain, simple, and easy to understand that even wayfaring men could not err in understanding. You would literally have to *want* not to understand.

In Matthew 13 the disciples asked Jesus why He spoke in parables. He said, "I speak to them in parables, because seeing they do not see, and hearing they do not hear, nor do they understand" (v. 13). But listen to Him in verse 15:

> For the hearts of this people have grown dull.
> Their ears are hard of hearing,
> And their eyes they have closed,
> Lest they should see with their eyes, and hear with their
> ears,
> Lest they should understand with their hearts and turn,
> So that I should heal them.

Jesus said a man would have to close his eyes, his spiritual eyes, to be able not to see the truth. A man would have to stop up his ears to be able not to hear or understand the simple truth of the gospel. Someone may say, "I don't understand it" or "I can't see the way you are preaching it." Why do you not understand it? Why can you not see it? Is it because you do not want to see it or is it because you need some guidance in seeing it?

Would God give His Son to die on the cross for the sins of the world, reveal His plan of salvation in the Bible, and then make it so confusing and complicated that we cannot understand it? That is not the God of the Bible. Men are not going to be lost because they cannot understand it or because God does not love them. Every soul is loved by God. "God demonstrates His own love toward us, in that while we were still sinners, Christ died for us" (Romans 5:8). Remember, no one wants you to be saved more than God does.

Suppose someone murdered one of your children with a rifle. Would you be able to say to him, "God bless you, sir. Is there anything I can do to help you?" The hardest thing I could ever do would be to say to someone who had taken the life of my son, "God bless you. Can I help you?" But that is what God did. Our sins crucified Him, but God says to us in essence, "I will bless you. I want to help you and save you." Oh, what a wonderful love our Father has for us.

My Need for the Answer

Let us return to the question, "Sirs, what must I do to be saved?" In order to read, answer, and respond, we must recognize our needs. We have to see ourselves as sinners in God's sight. We need to be like Peter when, after he had fished all night and caught nothing, complained about casting the nets one more time. But when he had to seek help to haul in the catch, he fell down at Jesus' feet with great apology: "Depart from me, for I am a sinful man" (Luke 5:8). We are all sinners (Romans 3:23).

Isaiah said, "All we like sheep have gone astray; we have turned, every one, to his own way; and the Lord has laid on Him the iniquity of us all" (Isaiah 53:6). We have to see ourselves as sinners, and that is a difficult task.

That reminds me of a man who responded to the invitation one Sunday morning. When the preacher asked him why he responded, the man replied, "I didn't come forward because of my sins. I came to pray for the sins of the church." That man was not ready to be saved, was he?

Before we are really ready to come to grips with this question, we must be willing to kneel at the foot of the cross. The Bible says that "God resists the proud, but gives grace to the humble" (1 Peter 5:5). The reason many never come to Christ is because of pride. They have too much pride to say, "I know I need the Lord in my life." Pride will keep you out of heaven.

In order to come to grips with the question, "what must I do to be saved?" we must be willing to put aside anything or anyone who would come between us and the Lord—pride, position, wealth, children, spouse, or any obstacles. The Bible says, "Whoever of you does not forsake all that he has cannot be My disciple" (Luke 14:33). That simply means we must not allow any relationship to keep us from Christ. We may have habits we must give up to come to Christ. We have to sacrifice ourselves when we come to the foot of the cross.

Repetition of the Greatest Question

"What must I do to be saved?" is asked three times in the book of Acts. Peter preached on the first Pentecost following the resurrection of Christ. He truthfully accused the audience regarding their actions toward Jesus: "You have taken by lawless hands, have crucified, and put to death" (Acts 2:23). They were cut to the heart and asked, "Men and brethren, what shall we do?" This is the first time this question was asked in the book of Acts.

The second instance is in Acts 9. Saul of Tarsus was on his way to Damascus to persecute Christians. Notice what happened:

> Then he fell to the ground, and heard a voice saying to him, "Saul, Saul, why are you persecuting Me?" And he said, "Who are You, Lord?" Then the Lord said, "I am Jesus, whom you are persecuting. It is hard for you to kick against the goads." So he, trembling and astonished, said, "Lord, what do You want me to do?" Then the Lord said to him, "Arise and go into the city, and you will be told what you must do" (Acts 9:4–6),

"What shall we do?" was first asked in Acts 2. Later in Acts 9, we hear Saul of Tarsus saying, "What do you want me to do?" In Acts 16 the Philippian jailer asked, "Sirs, what must I do to be saved?" (v. 30). Let us look at the answers given on these three occasions. A different answer is given in each case, and there is a good reason for that.

When Paul and Silas were fastened in stocks in an inner prison in Philippi, an earthquake occurred. Their chains were loosed and the prison doors opened. The jailer drew his sword to take his own life. However, Paul said, "Do yourself no harm, for we are all here" (Acts 16:28). Falling down before them, the man asked, "Sirs, what must I do to be saved?" He was a pagan and an unbeliever. What would be the first thing to tell an unbeliever who inquired about salvation? "Believe on the Lord Jesus Christ, and you will be saved, you and your household" (v. 31). The pagan jailer was told that in order to be saved he must believe on Jesus Christ.

Answers in Action

But how does an individual become a believer? We know from Romans 10:17 that faith comes by hearing, which comes by the word of God. Obviously, if this man is to become a believer, he must be taught. Notice the next verse:

> And they spoke the word of the Lord to him and to all that were in his house. And he took them the same hour of the night and washed their stripes. And immediately he and all his family were baptized (Acts 16:32–33).

So the question was, "What must I do to be saved?" and he was told, "Believe on the Lord Jesus Christ, and you will be saved, you and your household."

In Acts 2 the question was asked in a very similar way: "Men and brethren, what shall we do?" How did Peter answer this question? "Repent, and let every one of you be baptized in the name of Jesus Christ for the remission of sins; and you shall receive the gift of the Holy Spirit." So in response to "What shall we do?" they were told to repent and be baptized.

In Acts 9 Saul of Tarsus asked, "Lord, what do you want me to do?" (v. 6) Up to this point, Saul had persecuted those of the Way, the followers of Christ. But the Lord did not answer his question. Rather, He told him to go into the city and there he would find the answer.

In Acts 22 Paul is before an angry mob rehearsing the details of his conversion. He tells them what he was told to do in response to his question, "What shall I do, Lord?" (v. 10). At the time Saul asked that question, he was in conversation with Jesus and had just become a penitent believer. According to the Lord's instructions, Saul went into Damascus to await a messenger. He was taken to the house of Judas on Straight Street where he fasted and prayed to God for three days. At the end of that time, God sent Ananias to him. In response to the question Saul had asked the Lord on the Damascus highway, Ananias said to him, "And now why are you waiting? Arise and be baptized, and wash away your sins, calling on the name of the Lord" (v. 16).

The State of the Inquirer

Someone may say, "Brother Lambert, you've got me confused. Why would there be three answers to the same question?" Here's the answer.

Suppose you decide to take a hundred-mile trip. After traveling twenty-five miles, you stop and ask, "How far is it to my destination?"

The service station attendant replies, "About seventy-five miles."

You drive a little farther and then stop and ask, "How far is it to my destination?"

"About fifty miles," an old man on roadside tells you.

So you drive a little farther. Again, you stop and ask, "How far is it to my destination?" The same question, right?

The farmer in his fruit stand says, "About twenty-five miles."

What's happening? Why would you get three different answers to the same question? You know the answer: "Brother Lambert, it is because every time I asked the question I had progressed a little farther down the road." That is right. That is also the case in these three examples of conversion.

When the jailor in Acts 16 asked "what must I do to be saved?" he was at the beginning point of his journey to salvation. In Acts 2 the Pentecostians were past the point of belief when they asked, "Men and brethren, what shall we do?" They already knew who Jesus was; they needed to be told to repent of their sins. So they were told "repent and be baptized" to receive the blessing of salvation. But in Acts 22 Saul was told, "Arise and be baptized and wash away your sins." Why was he told this? Because he had already progressed further down the road of salvation. He had come to the point of belief and repentance and needed to know what to do next.

In all three examples, the inquirers were baptized. The reason there was a different answer was that they were each at a different stage of their development and understanding of what needed to be done in order to be saved. These three examples combined tell us what one must do in order to be saved. The sinner must believe on the Lord Jesus Christ, repent of his sins, and be baptized for the remission of those sins. Sins are washed away in the blood of the Lord Jesus Christ (Acts 22:16).

Conclusion

Jesus said in Mark 16:16, "He who believes and is baptized will be saved." You can be saved right now. I urge you to think seriously about that. One reason is because of our influence on each other. No man lives to himself, and no man dies to himself.

Another reason is that not a single one of us has a perpetual lease on life. Most of us will die before we intend. The Lord is coming back someday, and we do not know when. I plead with you not to wait, not even for a few days. It is not going to be easier later on because you have plenty of time. The one thing you do not have is plenty of time.

In the book of Proverbs, Solomon said, "Do not boast about tomorrow, for you do not know what a day may bring forth" (27:1). If I could impress anything on you, it would be to become a Christian now. I remember being in Trinidad in 1974. I was talking to a man at our crusade who was wrestling with the decision. I said, "How do you spell now?"

He responded, "Sir?"

I said again, "How do you spell now?"

He said, "N-O-W."

I replied, "Now, spell it backwards."

He looked at me rather quizzically, but said, "W-O-N."

I said, "If you will do it now, you will have the battle won."

9

Why Be a Christian?

The distinctive plea of the church of Christ is for a return to the authority of the Scriptures. We are pleading with honest men and women to speak where the Bible speaks and to be silent where the Bible is silent (1 Corinthians 4:6). We urge men to lay aside the shackles of human doctrines and opinions and just obey the Lord (1 Peter 4:11; 2 John 9; Revelation 22:18–19). We call men back to the old paths (Jeremiah 6:16).

By going back to the Bible, we can become what God wants us to be—Christians. A Christian is a disciple of the Lord (Acts 11:26). A Christian is one who is persuaded (Acts 26:28). A Christian is one who is willing to suffer for doing right (1 Peter 4:16).

Faithful Christians have given themselves to another and are no longer their own (1 Corinthians 6:19–20; 2 Corinthians 8:5; Romans 12:1–2).

Why should we be Christians?

The Only Way of True Happiness

You should want to be a Christian because God's way is the only way of true happiness. There is a lot of unhappiness in today's world. Unhappiness accounts for so many of our social problems, such as broken marriages and the success of the alcohol industry.

We do well to contrast the Christian life with the life of sin. The way of the sinner is hard. The way of the Christian is one of peace and joy (Proverbs 13:15; Isaiah 26:3; Philippians 4:4; Acts 16:30–34).

Best for Your Soul

You should want to be a Christian because it is best for your soul. Few men give thought to the needs of the soul (Luke 12:20–21). We pamper our bodies but neglect the soul (Matthew 16:26). However, our bodies will decay but the soul lives on (Ecclesiastes 12:5–7).

The soul of man needs saving (Hebrews 10:39; James 1:21; James 5:19–20). The unsaved soul is in danger of hell fire (Matthew 25:41; John 8:21). The saved man is delivered from that danger (Mark 16:15–16; Acts 2:37–40).

God Will Hear Your Prayers

We should be Christians so God will hear our prayers. The God of heaven and earth is a prayer-hearing God (Psalm 65:2). Elijah prayed and the heavens were closed. He prayed again and the rain came. Hezekiah prayed and God sent His angels and destroyed 185,000 soldiers in the enemy's camp. Daniel prayed and God gave him power to interpret the king's dream.

For God to hear my prayers I must be in a right relationship with Him (Psalm 66:18; 1 Peter 3:12; James 5:16).

Wonderful Fellowship in the Church

You should be a Christian because of the wonderful fellowship found in the church. There are some things with which we have no fellowship. We have no fellowship with unrighteousness (2 Corinthians 6:14). There is no fellowship with the unfruitful works of darkness (Ephesians 5:11).

It's exciting to know that as a Christian you are in fellowship with saints all over the world (1 John 1:7; Acts 2:42). In the local congregation there must be a close tie of fellowship between saints. When one suffers all suffer. When one rejoices all rejoice. Our closest friends ought to be fellow Christians. There are no superior or inferior positions in the fellowship of believers.

One should never do anything to break this fellowship (2 Thessalonians 3:6).

Simply a Christian

It is not our duty to be more than a Christian. Our only duty is to obey the Lord in all things (Ecclesiastes 12:13). A failure to obey the Lord will result in one's exclusion from heaven's door (Revelation 22:14). The New Testament disciples were not Pharisee Christians or Sadducee Christians. They were simply Christians (Acts 11:26).

The name Christian is not a nickname. God gave this name. In Acts 11:26 "were called" means "divinely instructed." "The Gentiles shall see your righteousness, and all kings your glory. You shall be called by a new name, which the mouth of the Lord will name" (Isaiah 62:2).

Only the seed makes Christians. The word of God is the seed of the kingdom (Luke 8:11; 1 Peter 1:23). Seed produces after its kind. This is true in the material creation (Genesis 1:12). This is also true in the spiritual realm. Suppose the game of baseball ceased for two hundred years and all rules of the game were lost. Then one day someone finds a rule book. If participants follow that rule book, then the game, exactly as we know it, could be played.

When men follow God's word—sow the seed of the kingdom—it can produce only what it produced in New Testament days—simply Christians. Suppose the Bible should be lost for hundreds of years and all traces of Christianity removed from the earth. Then one day in the far-distant future someone finds a copy of the Bible, reads it, and attempts to do what it says. What would it make of that person except a Christian?

You live a faithful Christian life by being just a Christian. Early saints such as Peter and Paul were just Christians. The Bible can make a Christian of anyone, anytime, anywhere.

Conclusion

There is more to being a Christian than living in a so-called Christian nation, having your name on the church roll, having Christian parents, or sitting in a meeting house three times a week.

You need to become a Christian today because it is best for your home (Joshua 24:15); because of the value of your soul (Matthew 16:26); because of the brevity of life (James 4:13–14).

SERMON

10

The Great Physician

Is there no balm in Gilead, is there no physician there? Why then is there no recovery for the health of the daughter of my people? (Jeremiah 8:22).

Jesus answered and said to them, "Those who are well have no need of a physician, but those who are sick. I have not come to call the righteous, but sinners, to repentance" (Luke 5:31–32).

Both of these scriptures, one from the Old Testament and one from the New, refer to Jesus as the physician of the soul or the great physician. The late Marshall Keeble referred to Jesus as being the doctor who never lost a case. But before anyone can see the need for a physician, he must first know he is sick.

The World Is Sick

Our world is sick. It is sick with an illness worse than yellow fever, the disease that took ten percent of Philadelphia's population in one month. It is worse than polio, the crippling disease that was especially active in the United States in the middle of last century. It is worse than cancer, the disease that takes the lives of so many of our loved ones every year. It is worse than heart disease, which strikes down so many Americans every year. This dreaded illness is a disease of the soul called sin. Our world is eaten up with sin.

In Isaiah 1:4, the prophet addressed problems of his day in speaking to God's people:

> Alas, sinful nation, a people laden with iniquity,
> A brook of evildoers, children who are corrupters!
> They have forsaken the Lord,
> They have provoked to anger The Holy One of Israel,
> They have turned away backward.

Then he continues in verses 5–6,

> Why should you be stricken again?
> You will revolt more and more.
> The whole head is sick, and the whole heart faints.
> From the sole of the foot even to the head,
> There is no soundness in it,
> But wounds and bruises and putrefying sores.

Isaiah describes God's people as if they were one great ulcer or spiritual sore. Yet in the midst of all of that, God showed His mercy:

> "Come now, and let us reason together," says the Lord, "though your sins be as scarlet, they shall be as white as snow; though they are red like crimson, they shall be as wool" (Isaiah 1:18).

So there was hope from God in spite of their despicable sin disease. The world is no different today than it was in the time of Isaiah.

> Young John Simmons finished medical school and set out to launch his practice in a small rural community. Doctor Simmons nervously awaited his first patient, knowing that a mistake with the first one could well mean there would not be a second one. He didn't have to wait long. Very soon after the office doors opened, Willie Johnson, a meticulous vegetable farmer entered and filled out his form. A few minutes later in the examination room, asked Willie, "How do you feel today, Mr. Johnson?"
>
> "I ain't feeling none too good," Willie said. "I wouldn't be wasting my time here if I was."
>
> "Have you ever had this problem before?" he said, as sympathetically as he knew how.
>
> "Yes, I have. One time."
>
> "Well, I hate to tell you, but you have it again."

Unclean!

The problem that we have in the world today is the same problem that we have been having since time began. It is called sin. Sin has been referred to by some as "leprosy of the soul." Leprosy seems to be a type of sin. Under Moses' law, leprosy caused uncleanness, not only to those who had the disease, but also to those who touched a diseased person or touched what a diseased person had touched! The leper was obligated to shout "unclean, unclean" when someone approached him. Sin makes us unclean.

When Isaiah received the call to the prophetic office in Isaiah 6, he was caught up in a vision in the throne room of God. In that perfect environment he cried out, "I am a man of unclean lips, and I dwell in the midst of a people of unclean lips" (Isaiah 6:5). He felt unworthy in the presence of God.

David wrote several psalms about his sin—psalms of penitence. He asked God for cleansing. In Psalm 51:10 he says, "Create in me a clean heart, O God, and renew a steadfast spirit within me." He knew that sin made him unclean in the sight of God.

Leprosy was not inherited. It could not be passed genetically from father to son. Neither is sin inherited. "The soul who sins shall die. The son shall not bear the guilt of the father, nor the father bear the guilt of the son" (Ezekiel 18:20).

Leprosy was not curable except by divine intervention. Luke 4:27 tells us "many lepers were in Israel in the time of Elisha the prophet, and none of them was cleansed except Naaman the Syrian." Of course, God intervened. He told Naaman through Elisha to dip seven times in the Jordan. Likewise, sin is incurable expect by the power of God.

What Can Wash Away My Sin?

"Is there no balm in Gilead? Is there no physician there?" (Jeremiah 8:22). The answer? "Yes there is." Hebrews 9:22 tells us that apart from the shedding of blood, there is no remission.

What can wash away my sin? The answer that we sometimes sing in response to that question is "Nothing but the blood of Jesus." Nothing but the blood of Jesus can give you access to God. There are a lot of things to which we have no access. For example, I do not have access to the Governor of Alabama. I cannot just pick up the telephone and say, "Governor, how are you doing?" I do not have access to the President of the United States. But let me tell you something that is thrilling. It is thrilling to know that we can have direct access to God! But that access comes only through the blood of our Lord.

> Therefore remember that you, once Gentiles in the flesh—who are called Uncircumcision by what is called the Circumcision made in the flesh by hands—that at that time you were without Christ, being aliens from the commonwealth of Israel and strangers from the covenants of promise, having no hope and without God in the world. But now in Christ Jesus you who once were far off have been brought near by the blood of Christ. For He Himself is our peace, who is made both one, and has broken down the middle wall of separation, having abolished in His flesh the enmity, that is, the law of commandments contained in ordinances, so as to create in Himself one new man from the two, thus making peace, and that He might reconcile them both to God in one body through the cross, thereby putting to death the enmity. And He came and preached peace to you who were afar off and to those who were near. For through Him we both have access by one Spirit to the Father (Ephesians 2:11–18).

The only way you will have access to God Almighty is through the Great Physician and the blood that was shed on Calvary.

On the Day of Atonement, the high priest performed all the rituals in the tabernacle. The tabernacle was a tent, designed by God, divided into two compartments. One was called the Holy Place, while the other was called the Most Holy Place. The High Priest was the only person permitted to enter the Most Holy Place, and then only on the Day of Atonement. On that day he offered an animal sacrifice for his sins, the sins of his family, and the sins of the people. Also on that day he sprinkled blood on the Mercy Seat, the dwelling place of God. The cleansing of the Mercy Seat made possible God's continued presence among His people.

Hebrews 10:3–4 tells us it is not possible for the blood of bulls and goats to take away sin. It also tells us that there was made a remembrance of sin every year. They rolled their sins forward every year. The priest would have to go in on the Day of Atonement the next year and repeat the process.

But here is good news. When the Lord Jesus Christ died on the cross, He opened the way for all men to have access to God Almighty—through His precious blood. Nothing but the blood of Jesus Christ can help us in the victory over the power of sin.

Zechariah 13:1 reveals another prophesy. "In that day a fountain shall be opened for the house of David and for the inhabitants of Jerusalem, for sin and for uncleanliness." A familiar song reminds of us this passage:

> There is a fountain filled with blood,
> Drawn from Emmanuel's veins;
> And sinners plunged beneath that flood
> Lose all their guilty stains.

Only through the blood of Christ can we become victorious over sin. In Matthew 26:28 Jesus said, "For this is My blood of the new covenant, which is shed for many for the remission of sins."

Jesus Saves

Preachers and Bible teachers sometimes use words with special meanings, assuming people understand them. Sometimes we assume too much. Consider the following words and phrases that we use frequently and see how they define God's treatment for sin.

- *Saved.* Mark 16:16 says, "He who believes and is baptized will be saved." *Saved* is used throughout the Bible.

- *Forgiveness.* Paul uses that word in Colossians 1:14: "In whom we have redemption through His blood, the forgiveness of sins."

- *Remission.* We understand that word as it pertains to our physical bodies. For example, if a cancer patient is successfully treated, we say the cancer is in remission. That means the cancer has been arrested and is no longer growing in the person's body. The Lord is in the remission business. In Acts 2:38 Peter said, "Repent, and let every one of you be baptized in the name of Jesus Christ for the remission of sins."

- *Covered.* Psalm 32:1 says, "Blessed is he whose transgression is forgiven, whose sin is covered."

- *Blotted out.* Acts 3:19 Peter says, "Repent therefore and be converted, that your sins may be blotted out."

- *Remember no more.* In Hebrews 8:12 we read, "For I will be merciful to their unrighteousness, and their sins and their lawless deeds I will remember no more."

Let us think about all these expressions: *saved, forgiveness, covered, remission, blotted out,* and *remember no more.* They all mean the same thing. The only way we have access to the blessings suggested by those words and phrases is through the blood of the Lord Jesus Christ. Nothing but the blood can help us win the victory over the power of sin.

The Blood-Bought Church

Nothing but the blood can make the church possible. I often hear the expression, "You have a pretty church." I think this too. I believe they are the most beautiful people I have ever seen, but our well-wishers are talking about the building. And sometimes we use the same accommodative language. However, the church is the people, not the building.

The Bible sometimes speaks of the church in someone's house. We read of Paul making "havoc of the church, entering every house, and dragging off men and women, committing them to prison" (Acts 8:3). The church is composed of people who have been blood redeemed.

> And one of the elders answered, saying to me, "Who are those arrayed in white robes, and where did they come from?" And I said to him, "Sir, you know." So he said to me, "These are the ones who came out of the great tribulation, and washed their robes and made them white in the blood of the Lamb" (Revelation 7:13–14).

The church is made up of people who are blood washed.

We also have been bought.

Or do you not know that your body is the temple of the Holy Spirit who is in you, whom you have from God, and you are not your own? For ye are bought at a price; therefore glorify God in your body and in your spirit, which are God's (1 Corinthians 6:19–20).

We are God's. We are blood-bought people.

Therefore take heed to yourselves and to all the flock, among which the Holy Spirit has made you overseers, to shepherd the church of God which he purchased with His own blood (Acts 20:28).

Nothing but the blood can make the church possible.

The Church—Purposed and Promised

The church was eternally purposed (Ephesians 3:10–11). The church was prophetically foretold. Daniel 2:44 says,

And in the days of these kings the God of heaven will set up a kingdom which shall never be destroyed; and the kingdom shall not be left to other people; it shall break in pieces and consume all these kingdoms, and it shall stand for ever.

This is a prophesy of the coming of the kingdom of God, the church. It was faithfully promised. When Jesus came into Caesarea Philippi, He made this promise: "And I also say to you that you are Peter, and on this rock I will build My church, and the gates of Hades shall not prevail against it" (Matthew 16:18).

The church was established on the first Pentecost after the resurrection of Christ. Acts 2 gives a historical account of how the church began that day.

What made all of this possible? Nothing but the blood.

Overcoming Daily Struggles

The everyday Christian life strengthens every member, and I need strength. I need something to give me power, to give me strength, and to give me help in living the Christian life every day. I need to be reminded that there is a way for me to fight the devil every day. As a Christian, you too are going to be fighting the devil every day. How do you do that? Nothing but the blood.

Revelation 12 tells us about spiritual warfare. How did the early saints overcome the devil? Read verse 11: "And they overcame him by the blood of the Lamb and by the word of their testimony, and they did not love their lives to the death." The way you defeat the devil is through the power of the blood of the Lord Jesus Christ!

The Blood Keeps You Clean

Christians, pay attention to a verse of hope and assurance— a verse of victory! "If we walk in the light as He is in the light, we have fellowship with one another, and the blood of Jesus Christ His Son cleanses us from all sin" (1 John 1:7). How many of our sins? *All* of them. When you walk in that light and are living a dedicated Christian life to the best of your ability and knowledge, the blood of Jesus Christ keeps you clean.

When I was a young Christian, I was correctly taught that a Christian could get out of the light, but I was not thoroughly instructed about walking in the light. Now we all need someone to tell us how to stay in the light. I know that if I walk in that light as He is in the light, I have the blood of Jesus Christ continually cleansing me. You mean I am perfect? I am not suggesting that. If I were perfect, I would not need the blood, would I? It is because of my imperfections that I need it.

Have you ever cut your hand and bled a bit? Of course you have. And when you do get cut, you actually need to bleed a little. Do you know why? It rids the cut of impurities. In a similar way, when the spiritual body is wounded, when a Christian messes up and asks God to forgive him, Jesus' blood keeps cleansing him of his sins. If you do not believe that, then you do not believe the Holy Spirit. You do not believe God. You do not believe Jesus. You do not believe the Bible. And, most likely, you are not walking in the light. Nothing but the blood can keep you clean.

The Blood Gives You Access to Heaven

Nothing but the blood is going to give you access to heaven. Look at Hebrews 9:12: "Not with the blood of goats and calves, but with His own blood He entered the Most Holy Place once for all, having obtained eternal redemption." Do you know what that Most Holy Place is? It is heaven. When Jesus died on the cross, the veil in the temple was ripped from top to bottom signifying that the way into the Most Holy Place (heaven) had been opened for all mankind. Sometimes we sing "The Way of the Cross Leads Home." That is true. Nothing but the blood can do that.

A Clean Conscience

What washes away our sins? Let God answer that: "To Him who loved us and washed us from our sins in His own blood" (Revelation 1:5). What will give us remission of sins? Again, let God again answer that: "For this is My blood of the new covenant, which is shed for many for the remission of sins" (Matthew 26:28).

What can give me a clean conscience?

> Not with the blood of goats and calves, but by His own blood He entered the Most Holy Place once for all, having obtained eternal redemption. For if the blood of bulls and goats and the ashes of a heifer, sprinkling the unclean, sanctifies for the purifying of the flesh, how much more shall the blood of Christ, who through the eternal Spirit offered Himself without spot to God, cleanse your conscience from dead works to serve the living God? (Hebrews 9:12–14).

What does this mean? The only way I will have a clean, purged conscience is through the blood of the Lord Jesus Christ. Do you feel guilty? You need the blood of Christ.

Why Are You Waiting?

How do I get in touch with the blood? How can I have my sins washed away? God has the answer to those questions. "And now why are you waiting? Arise and be baptized, and wash away your sins, calling on the name of the Lord" (Acts 22:16). Also in Acts 2:38 Peter said, "Repent, and let every one of you be baptized in the name of Jesus Christ for the remission of sins; and you shall receive the gift of the Holy Spirit." Why repent and be baptized? For the remission of sin!

What can give me a clean conscience? Nothing but the blood (Hebrews 9:14). When does the blood of the Lord do that for me? Ponder the words of Peter:

There is also an antitype which now saves us—baptism (not the removal of the filth of the flesh, but the answer of a good conscience toward God), through the resurrection of Jesus Christ (1 Peter 3:21).

We need to have a good conscience toward God. In order to do that, we have to come to where the blood is found. Jesus is the physician of the soul.

Why Not Come to the Physician?

Why is it so difficult to get people to come to Christ? Admittedly, we do live in an unusual time. If you were a Christian forty years ago, you can remember scores of people walking down the aisles at meetings. Thirty-five years ago, the church of Christ was the fastest growing religious body in the United States. We were number one because we were preaching the gospel. But today is a different time and age.

Why don't more people come to the Great Physician? What excuses do they offer?

1. *I am not sick.* Some may believe they have no spiritual defects. People sometimes ask me, "Are you okay?" and I respond "I'm fine." "Are you sure?" they ask. Then I began to wonder if I look pale—if I have symptoms I have not picked up on. Spiritually sick people are everywhere, and many of them don't even know it. They do not think they need Jesus.

2. *My condition is not serious.* Some know they are not spiritually well, but they do not think their sickness is serious. I remember a young man whose wedding ceremony I had performed. I learned that a few months into the marriage, he made his wife strip in the presence of another man while he beat her with a belt. I suppose it would not surprise you to hear that she left him. He mourned for a week and then took another woman from a man and moved her into his house. The elders tried to catch up with him. It was like trying to catch a rabbit that was on the run. When they finally found him, he was rather obstinate, to say the least. They informed him that his scandalous actions were known to all in the church as well as

the small community, and that they had no choice but to withdraw their fellowship publicly from him. I requested of the elders, "Let me go see him first. I feel some responsibility because I baptized him and preformed the wedding ceremony." I thought perhaps his grandmother, a godly saint, could help to affect a change for good in his life.

"Do you realize how serious this is?" I said to him.

He hedged: "I don't think it's all that bad."

"Well, let me tell you how bad it is," I pleaded. "It is so bad that unless you repent, you will lose your soul."

I continued, "You don't love the woman you have moved into this house." She was in the other room not saying very nice things about me. I could hear her.

I continued, "The only reason you have her in this house is to satisfy your fleshly desires. If you really love her, you'll get her out of here."

His response? "You go and do what you've got to do."

So I did. In his mind, his sin was not serious. However, he and God did not see eye-to-eye. Sin demanded the very life of God's Son, so it is no joke or pleasure to Him. The cross is a testimony to God's hatred for sin.

3. *I don't like the medicine.* Some do not come to Jesus because they don't want to take the medicine. Have you ever gone to the doctor, paid him your hard-earned money, had a prescription filled, taken a few doses, and then just put it on the shelf where it would be "out of sight, out of mind"? Then did you wonder why you never got well? No. You know why. You did not take the medicine.

A woman, seriously ill, went to the doctor. He gave her a prescription and urged her to follow the directions. A few days later she was found dead in bed. The medicine was on her nightstand—unopened. She ignored that which would have saved her life. In John 5:40 Jesus said, "But you are not willing to come to me that you may have life."

4. *I'll make my own medicine.* Many will not accept Jesus' prescription because they are taking a more familiar

"homemade remedy." Rather than asking, "Lord, what would you have me to do?" they are asking God to respond favorably to the foreign schemes and ideas they have come up with and grant them salvation. God has never promised salvation through a "homemade remedy," even if it was concocted by someone who has the appearance of spirituality.

5. *I'll go to the doctor later.* Some are not saved because they wait too late to go to the doctor. I have visited hospitals many times because families wanted me, their preacher, to be by their side during difficult times. It is not unusual for a family member to follow me from the patient's room to a private place to relay the words of the doctor: "There's nothing more I can do." But the saddest of these stories end with these words from the doctor: "Had he come to me just two weeks sooner, the situation would be very different now." How sad to deal with families grieving for those who waited until it was too late to see the doctor.

But remember this: you can also wait too late to come to the Great Physician. Stop procrastinating. The time to come is now.

> Two men were walking down a country road, arguing as they went along. They disagreed about the best time of the year to cut a hickory stick. One said the best time was in the springtime. The other said the best time was in the fall. They spotted a farmer out in his pasture, went over to the fence, and called him. "Settle an argument for us, sir. What is the best time to cut a hickory stick?"
>
> Without changing his expression the old farmer said, "The best time to cut a hickory stick is when you find it."

The best time to come to Jesus is right now.

11

The Resurrection:
Our Glorious Hope

"Then they went in and did not find the body of the Lord Jesus" (Luke 24:3). What happened to Jesus' body? No one ever found the body of Jesus. And His grave is still without a tenant. The resurrection of Jesus Christ is a fact of great spiritual significance. For if His resurrection is disproved, Christianity will become powerless. So let's study the resurrection of Jesus Christ.

Life beyond the Grave

From his creation, man has been religious. All men throughout the ages have recognized the existence of the higher power. It may have been the sun, the moon, or the stars, but man has always worshiped something. Also, men have always anticipated life beyond the grave. For the American Indian, it was the happy hunting ground, so the warrior's bow and arrows were buried with him. His distorted view does not nullify his claim that a future life exists. All men—the savage and the civilized, the educated and the uneducated—have had some anticipation of life beyond the grave. God has so designed man that his innate belief of eternal life is inevitable. Even the infidel, in view of death and the grave, testifies that a future life is possible. Colonel Robert Ingersoll was once asked to speak at the graveside of an infant. He betrayed his infidelity that day:

> My friends, I know how vain it is to gild a grief with words. And yet I wish to take from every grave its fears. Here in this world where life and death are equal kings, all should be brave enough to meet what all have met. From the tree of life buds and blossoms fall with ripened fruit, and in the common bed of earth, babes and patriarchs sleep side by side. Why should we fear that which will come to all that is? We cannot say that death is not good. We do not know whether death is the end of life or the door of another. Every cradle asks us, "Whence?" and every coffin, "Wither?"

In view of the grave, even the unbeliever says it must be possible.

The question that has been on the hearts of men through the centuries is recorded in Job 14:14: "If a man dies, shall he live again?" The answer must come from every informed person. Yes, man will live again. And our hope in life beyond the grave comes through the Lord Jesus Christ. Friends, the Bible teaches a future resurrection of the human body. Consider the following verses:

> Your dead shall live; together with my dead body they shall arise. Awake and sing, you who dwell in dust; for your dew is like the dew of herbs, and the earth shall cast out the dead (Isaiah 26:19).

> For I know that my Redeemer lives, and He shall stand at last on the earth: and after my skin is destroyed, this I know, that in my flesh I shall see God (Job 19:25–26).

> Many of those who sleep in the dust of the earth shall awake, some to everlasting life, some to shame and everlasting contempt (Daniel 12:2).

> Do not marvel at this; for the hour is coming, in which all who are in the graves will hear His voice and come forth—those who have done good, to the resurrection of life, and those who have done evil, to the resurrection of condemnation (John 5:28–29).

> I am the resurrection and the life. He who believes in Me, though he may die, he shall live. (John 11:25).

And then in that great resurrection chapter of the Bible, 1 Corinthians 15, Paul writes,

Behold, I tell you a mystery: We shall not all sleep, but we shall all be changed—in a moment, in the twinkling of an eye, at the last trumpet. For the trumpet will sound, and the dead will be raised incorruptible, and we shall be changed. For this corruptible must put on incorruption, and this mortal must put on immortality. So when this corruptible has put on incorruption, and this mortal has put no immortality, then shall be brought to pass the saying that is written: "Death is swallowed up in victory" (1 Corinthians 15:51–54).

Yes, the Bible teaches a future resurrection of the dead, and any individual who goes home to heaven beyond the grave will go there because the Lord Jesus Christ was raised from the dead and because that individual accepts the doctrine of the resurrection gospel. And make no mistake about it. God Almighty has the power to raise the dead. Paul said, "According to the working of His mighty power which he worked in Christ when He raised Him from the dead" (Ephesians 1:19).

God's Power to Raise the Dead

God showed His power when He raised His Son from the dead. We live in a marvelous age, and I appreciate those who have made it possible. I believe we live in the best of times and the worst of times. Some things about our lives today have degenerated, haven't they? But those of you in your sixties, did you ever think you would see men in outer space? Did you, when you were in your early teens, think a man would walk on the moon? I certainly didn't, but by way of television, we all have. I do remember one poor woman, now deceased, who believed all our space exploration to be a Hollywood stunt—the "space craft" actually landed in the desert somewhere in west Texas. But I'm convinced that Neil Armstrong and others actually walked on the moon. But have you ever thought about this? If one of those men had died there, no scientist, no engineer, and no physician on the face of the earth could have brought him back to life. But God Almighty has that power.

Almost two thousand years ago, His Son came into this world and lived a life of poverty and rejection. He was eventually taken by lawless men, crucified, and slain. His body was taken from that cross and put into a borrowed tomb—a new tomb. And three days later He came forth from that grave triumphant, having been raised by God's power. Matthew records these three words: "He is risen" (Matthew 28:6). Make no mistake about it—God Almighty has the power to raise the dead.

Keystone of Christianity

If an individual really believes the fact of Jesus' resurrection, it is much easier for that person to believe everything else about Jesus, including that He is who He claimed to be—the Son of God. Many years ago, I read a book on Christian evidences by J. W. McGarvey. In that book McGarvey said if he were to debate an atheist, he would debate him on the resurrection of Jesus Christ. Why? Because the evidence for the resurrection of Jesus Christ is overwhelming. And I'm glad of that. Why?

- If He has not been raised from the dead, we Christians are wasting our time honoring Him.
- If He has not been raised from the dead, the church doesn't have a foundation.
- If Jesus has not been raised from the dead, we have no salvation message.
- If Jesus has not been raised from the dead, we are dead in our sins.
- If Jesus has not been raised from the dead, we have no hope.
- If Jesus has not been raised from the dead, we are of all men most pitiable.

The entire fabric of Christianity is woven around an empty tomb!

The fact of Jesus' resurrection has its critics. Unbelievers have advanced many theories in an effort to discourage an investigation of the resurrection of our Lord.

The Swoon Theory

Some people believe that Jesus only appeared to be lifeless when He was taken down from the cross, but in the dampness of the tomb He revived and escaped.

I would ask this critic to watch the execution with me. We begin just outside Pilate's Hall.

Watch that expert scourger as he administers lashes to the Lord's back, beating it to a bloody pulp. We can hardly watch; the Prisoner us losing a lot of blood. At last the beating is finished, and the execution team, along with the accusers, is leaving Pilate's Hall. The centurion presses into service one called Simon to carry His cross, perhaps because the bloody Prisoner is not strong enough to bear it.

The execution team is arriving at the place of the skull with the Prisoner. The soldiers, without thought or hesitation, throw the Prisoner on the ground and drive five-inch spikes into His hands and feet. Now the crown of thorns! Tremendous pain! But no matter! He's a criminal who claimed to be a king, so some kind of crown is necessary.

See Him writhe in pain, suspended between heaven and earth, in a public place. "It is finished," He says. At last the indescribable agony is over. Watch that soldier plunging the spear into His side, all the way into His heart. Blood and water are pouring out! The blood has begun to coagulate. Jesus has been dead for a while.

Listen! A prominent member of the Sanhedrin is making a formal request of the procurator for the body of Jesus. I wish we could Pilate's face. His eyebrows are probably raised in surprise. *He's dead? He's dead already?* Pilate had to be sure. At his command, a courier fetches the centurion. We see that soldier, experienced in such matters, enter the hall and assure Pilate that Jesus has "been dead for some time" (Mark 15:44). Pilate then grants to Joseph of Arimathea the body of Jesus.

Let's go back to Golgotha. Under Joseph's watchful eye, the body is removed from the cross. Those men transport His body to a new tomb in a nearby garden. We'll stay here at a distance while the body is wrapped hurriedly, for the Sabbath is coming on. They must be finished before sundown.

At last Joseph and his men emerge from the tomb. Some of the strong men grasp a large wheel-like stone and roll it into place. The tomb is shut.

But we need to return here tomorrow for one more event. The chief priests and Pharisees are concerned about security. After all, the disciples might steal the body and claim He was resurrected. The leading Jews will have to confer with Pilate.

It's early now on the day after the crucifixion; we're back at the tomb. The chief priest and some of the Pharisees are approaching. They march directly to the stone, set a seal on it, and turn to give instructions to the captain of the guard. Then they depart. They have done what Pilate authorized: "Make it as secure as you know how" (Matthew 27:65).

Here's my question for the critic: If Jesus did not die, if He just fainted on the cross, how did He, in such a weakened physical condition, muster the strength to roll away that stone? And then having done that, how could He overcome those soldiers who would face the death penalty if they allowed their Prisoner to escape? I'll give you the answer to that. Not only did He die on that cross but He was also raised from the dead by the power of God.

The Stolen-Body Theory

Someone says, "Well, the enemies of Jesus stole the body." That's another theory. In the first place, what was their motive for taking the body? When Joseph put Jesus in that tomb, that's exactly where His enemies wanted Him. They had no motive to steal His body.

Second, there was a death penalty connected with tampering with a tomb. Can you imagine His enemies subjecting themselves to a death penalty just to take away the body of this man? They didn't have a motive for doing that.

When Peter stood up on Pentecost day fifty days later to preach that first recorded gospel sermon, some in his audience had played a pivotal role in our Lord's death. Do you know what he preached to those people? He preached that they had crucified the Son of God (Acts 2:23) and that He had been raised from the dead (Acts 2:24). And guess what? No one disputed it! Why didn't someone say, "No, He has not been raised. We have His body as evidence." They didn't say that because Jesus had been raised.

The Hallucination Theory

Someone says, "Well, the people just thought they saw Jesus." Some doubters say that those who claim they saw Jesus were hallucinating. It is true that sometimes people think they see things that don't really exist. I recall one Sunday morning on my way to a preaching appointment, driving up the interstate, in the distance I saw a man hitchhiking. But you know what happened as I got nearer to that hitchhiker? The image of the man became a sign. I had imagined a man in the distance.

So it is possible for people to imagine they see certain things. Two people might imagine the same thing, but in 1 Corinthians 15, Paul said that more than five hundred brethren at once saw Jesus after His death. Did all of them hallucinate? I think not! He was raised from the dead by the power of God!

The Resurrection in the Scriptures

My friend, the book I hold in my hand tells us that Jesus was raised from the dead by God's mighty power.

- *Psalm 16:10.* "For you will not leave my soul in Sheol; nor will you allow your Holy One to see corruption."

- *Acts 2:31.* "He, foreseeing this, spoke concerning the resurrection of the Christ, that His soul was not left in Hades [the unseen world] nor did His flesh see corruption."

- *Matthew 12:40.* For as Jonah was three days and three nights in the belly of the great fish, so will the Son of Man be three days and three nights in the heart of the earth.

- *Matthew 16:21.* Jesus told the disciples that He "must go to Jerusalem, and suffer many things at the hands of the chief priests and scribes, and be killed, and be raised again the third day."

- *Acts 2:24.* Peter said, "Whom God raised up, having loosed the pains of death, because it was not possible that He should be held by it."

- *Acts 17:30–31.* "Truly, these times of ignorance God overlooked, but now commands men everywhere to repent, because He has appointed a day on which He will judge the world in righteousness by the Man whom He has ordained. He has given assurance of this to all by raising Him from the dead" (Acts 17:30–31).

- *Romans 1:4.* "And declared to be the Son of God with power [he's talking about Jesus] according to the Spirit of holiness, by the resurrection from the dead."

- *Romans 4:25.* Jesus "was delivered up because of our offences, and was raised because of our justification."

- *Romans 6:4.* "Therefore we are buried with him through baptism into death, just as Christ was raised from the dead by the glory of the Father, even so we also should walk in newness of life."

- *Romans 10:9.* "That if thou confess with your mouth the Lord Jesus and believe in your heart that God has raised Him from the dead, you will be saved."

- *1 Corinthians 15:1–4.* "Moreover, brethren, I declare to you the gospel which I preached to you, which also you have received and in which you stand, by which also you are saved, if you hold fast that word which I preached to you—unless you believed in vain. For I delivered to you first of all that which I also received: that Christ died for our sins according to the Scriptures, and that He was buried, and that He rose again the third day according to the Scriptures."

What do all of those verses tell us? The Bible is testifying to the fact that Jesus Christ, the divine Son of God, lived, died, was buried, and was raised from the dead by the power of God.

Is the Resurrection Relevant Today?
Someone might say, "Brother Lambert, you've wasted a lot of our time because all of us believe that." And I hope you do believe it. Others may be wondering, "Why should we be thinking about it in the twenty-first century? Why should we be talking about something that happened almost two thousand years ago?

Death Has Not Conquered

One of the reasons we should to be concerned about Jesus' resurrection is because it tells us death is not the victor of life. Suppose I were to call on you tonight to give me a list of the world's greatest conquerors. You might name Caesar and Alexander and Hitler and Napoleon and maybe a lot of others. But I have an idea some would overlook the greatest conqueror of them all. He rides on a white horse and he flies a black flag. He digs a trench across the continents and the hemispheres of the world, filling it with the bodies of the young and the old, the rich and the poor, the black and the white, and the yellow and the red. And that conqueror's name is Death.

Often we are called to the graveside of someone we have loved dearly. When we stand beside that open tomb, if we're not careful, we may think like this, "Death has conquered." But friends, because God had the power to raise Jesus Christ from the dead, I know He has the power to raise us from the dead. And hence we can say with Paul, "Thanks be to God, who gives us the victory through our Lord Jesus Christ" (1 Corinthians 15:57). Death is not the champion that overcomes life. Because of Jesus, death is not the victor over life!

I Trust Jesus with My Soul

We need to be concerned about His resurrection because it tells me that He's the only one I can trust with my soul. There are a lot of people that I appreciate, that I admire.

As a lad of sixteen I began to think about preaching, so I remembered a book Dad had bought the year I was born. Incidentally, I still have that book, the purchase date carefully written on the title page: *The Life, Letters, and Sermons of T. B. Larimore.* I began immediately to study that book. T. B. Larimore must have been one of the greatest preachers of his time. It was not unusual for him to engage in a six-month preaching tour. I continue to admire his dedication, but T. B. Larimore didn't die for me. He wasn't raised from the dead that I might live.

I admire John the Baptist. He was the forerunner of Christ, wasn't he? And I'll tell you something. It would be a different world today if we had more preachers today with the courage of John the Baptist. But John didn't die for me. He wasn't raised from the dead that I might live.

I appreciate others who were instrumental in the movement to restore first century Christianity in the modern world. Men like James O'Kelly, Barton W. Stone, and Alexander and Thomas Campbell. But none of those men died for me. And not a one of them was ever raised from the dead for me. I can't trust them with my soul.

Jesus both died on the cross and was raised from the dead that you and I might live. In John 14:6 Jesus said, "I am the way, the truth, and the life. No one comes to the Father except through Me." And yet men in the religious world today are going to almost every source imaginable except the Lord Jesus Christ to find out what He would have them do. He's the only one you can trust.

The Goodness of God

And then we ought to be concerned about His resurrection, because His resurrection is the goodness of God to get us to live right: to get us to believe and to repent and to be baptized and to be faithful Christians. Romans 2:4 tells us that the goodness of God leads us to repentance.

We live in a sinful world, but no one knows that any better than God does. And no one has done any more about it than God has. He gave His Son.

The Resurrection Inspires Repentance

Luke records the parable about the rich man and Lazarus (cf. Luke 16). A certain rich man was clothed in purple and fine linen, and fared sumptuously every day. Lazarus, a poor beggar covered with sores, was laid at the rich man's gate, desiring the crumbs that fell from the rich man's table.

Both the rich man and Lazarus died. Then in the Hadean world, the suffering rich man asked Abraham to send Lazarus "that he may dip the tip of his finger in water and cool my tongue." Request denied, but the rich man didn't give up: "Send him to my father's house, for I have five brothers . . . lest they also come to this place of torment." Abraham replied, "They have Moses and the prophets; let them hear them." The rich man said, "No, father Abraham; but if one goes to them from the dead, they will repent" (Luke 16:30).

I don't have any idea what would have happened if Abraham had Lazarus back to that man's house, do you? But the rich man sincerely believed if Lazarus were resurrected his brothers would repent.

I want to tell you something. You and I have that resurrected one. We have Him who was raised from the dead that we might believe, that we might repent, that we might be baptized, that we might live a faithful, dedicated, Christian life. So when a person gets in a flippant way, turning his nose up at God and disobeying Him, that person had might as well shake his fist in God's face and say, "I don't care that Your Son died on that cross. I don't care that Your Son was raised from the dead." Oh, it was the goodness of God that commanded us to believe, repent, be baptized, and be faithful so we can be saved. We had better be concerned.

12

Oh, What a Savior

"And she will bring forth a Son, and you shall call His name Jesus, for He will save His people from their sins" (Matthew 1:21).

No life has so radically changed civilization as the life of Jesus Christ. Jesus gave us a new way of calculating time. He stands between BC and AD. We date our letters from the time of His birth.

Literature has been enriched because of the life of Jesus Christ. The art of the world would have been poorer had Jesus not lived. The status of women has been elevated because Jesus Christ came into this world. And yet Jesus Christ never traveled very far from His home. He never ran for a political office. He never wrote a book. He never made investments on Wall Street. He never hit a home run. He never stared in a movie. He never made a touchdown. Yet Jesus Christ stands out as the greatest person ever to live on this earth.

Friends, Jesus is wonderful. As a matter of fact, we learn that His name is "Wonderful" (Isaiah 9:6). That passage says, "For unto us a Child is born, unto us a Son is given; and the government will be upon His shoulder. And His name will be called Wonderful."

Not only is His name "Wonderful," Jesus is wonderful.

- *He is wonderful in life.* Acts 10:38 tells us that Jesus went about doing good.
- *He is wonderful in love.* In John 15:13 we're told, "Greater love has no one than this, than to lay down one's life for his friends."

- *He is wonderful in compassion.* In Matthew 9:36 when Jesus saw the people wandering about as sheep without a shepherd, He was moved with compassion.
- *He is wonderful in promises.* In 2 Peter 1:4 Peter describes Jesus' promises as being "exceedingly great and precious."
- *He is wonderful in power.* In Ephesians 3:20 Paul said He is "able to do exceedingly abundantly above all that we ask or think."
- *He is wonderful in purpose.* And His purpose is stated by Paul in 1 Timothy 1:15: "This is a faithful saying and worthy of all acceptance, that Christ Jesus came into the world to save sinners."

My Need for a Savior

Jesus Christ came into the world, sent by His Father. In John 4:34 Jesus Christ said, "My food is to do the will of Him who sent Me." Jesus Christ was sent to die. Second Corinthians 8:9 says, "For you know the grace of our Lord Jesus Christ, that though He was rich, yet for your sakes He became poor, that you through His poverty might become rich." Jesus Christ came into this world to be our Savior, and oh, what a Savior.

Mankind is in need of a Savior. All human efforts are feeble and ineffective in saving our souls.

- *Science cannot save our souls.* Science may put men out into space, but science cannot put men into heaven.
- *Technology cannot save our souls.* Technology may make our lives better, but technology cannot make our souls better.
- *Medicine cannot save our souls.* Medicine may help our bodies, but medicine cannot heal souls.
- *Wealth cannot save our souls.* Wealth may build houses, but wealth cannot build eternal homes.

The Sin Problem

All human efforts are futile when it comes to saving our souls. It was because of our predicament that God sent Jesus into the world to be our Savior. Man's dreaded predicament is sin. You can call it whatever you wish, but sin by any other name is still sin. Sin is described in 1 John 3:4 (KJV) as a "transgression of the law," that is, doing what God has forbidden. Sin is also described in James 4:17 as omission. We know to do good, and when we fail to do good we sin. First John 5:17 tells us that all unrighteousness is sin. Then in Romans 14:23 we learn that when we violate a biblically regulated conscience, we sin: "Whatever is not from faith is sin." James 2:9 also tells us that when we show respect of persons, we commit sin. Sin is a terrible monster, a very deceitful monster. In Hebrews 3:13 Paul tells us to take heed "lest any of you be hardened through the deceitfulness of sin."

Oh, sin is such a deceitful thing. It promises you life and gives you death. It promises you light and gives you darkness. It promises you joy and gives you sorrow. It promises you health and gives you sickness. It promises you freedom and gives you slavery. It promises you heaven and gives you hell.

Sin would have you believe it is your best friend, when in reality it is your worst enemy. Proverbs 13:15 says that the way of the transgressor is hard (KJV).

> A preacher went to a prison—not to be an inmate, although maybe some need to be—as a speaker to the inmates. As he walked past the first guard, and approached the first lock, he noticed these words above the door: "The way of transgressors is hard" (Proverbs 13:15 KJV).
>
> He turned aside to the warden: "You know, warden, you need to put those words on the outside so people out there will know that the way of the transgressor is hard."
>
> The warden answered, "Preacher, it is your job to tell people on the outside that the way of the transgressors is hard. But once they get past you, we want them to be reminded daily that it does not pay to violate the law."

- *Sin is a separator.* Yes, sin is our greatest enemy, because sin is a separator. Isaiah 59:2 says, "Your iniquities have separated you from your God; and your sins have hidden His face from you, so that He will not hear." Sin separates man from God. Sin separates nations. Sin separates families. Sin separates communities. Sin separates churches. And sin separates souls from God Almighty.

- *Sin pollutes.* This is one form of pollution you will not hear the environmentalists talking about—the pollution of the soul. In Psalm 51:10 when penitent David was asking for God's forgiveness, he said, "Create in me a clean heart, O God, and renew a steadfast spirit within me." David felt dirty because of his sin. That's what sin does to those who engage in it.

- *Sin scars.* If you drive a nail into the living room wall, your wife will not like it. So to please her, you remove it. What do you have as a result? A hole! And you can't pull out the hole. When we sin, God may forgive us, but the mark—the memory and effect of what we've done—remains on our hearts, and sometimes on society. Isn't that what David meant in Psalm 51:3 when he said, "My sin is always before me." He just couldn't forget what he had done.

- *Sin warps the mind.* We wonder why some maniacs are running around in some of our large cities shooting people. That's how sin affects the mind. You want to know why we've had some nuts running around all over our nation abducting little girls, and in some cases, killing them? It's because sin can permanently warp and twist the mind. Certain people can commit heinous crimes and never be troubled. That's what Paul meant in Romans 1:28 when he said, "God gave them over to a debased mind, to do those things which are not fitting."

- *Sin affects the will.* Sin wants you to think you're in control when in reality sin is in control. In other words, sin wants you to think you are the master when in reality sin is the master. That's just how sin can affect the will of man.

- *Sin hardens the conscience.* That's why a man can take a gun, aim it at a human being, and pull the trigger. A parolee from a Chicago prison once told me, "If you stay in prison long enough, killing a person doesn't mean any more to you and stepping on a bug." How can a man's heart get that way? Through sin! That's what sin does to a person. It hardens the conscience. Listen to Paul:

> Now the Spirit expressly says that in latter times some will depart from the faith, giving heed to deceiving spirits and doctrines of demons, speaking lies in hypocrisy, having their own conscience seared with a hot iron (1 Timothy 4:1).

When you sear the flesh of an animal—for example, when you brand a cow—the hot metal hardens the flesh. In a similar way, sin can harden the human heart. That's why sin is such a dangerous thing. It is time that we in America start calling sin by its right name. That is not fashionable but it is right. It might not be politically correct, but it is the right thing to do in the sight of God.

"Well," somebody says, "what do you think is the greatest thing we can do for people today?" The greatest thing we can do for the human race is to warn them of the danger of sin and the consequences of a life of sin. Oh, yes, we need a Savior. We need a Savior because of sin; because sin is a reality in the life of everyone. What a Savior we have! Oh, thank God we have such a Savior!

To Save Sinners

Jesus came to save sinners. Go back to Paul's statement in 1 Timothy 1:15: "This is a faithful saying and worthy of all acceptance, that Christ Jesus came into the world to save sinners." Did you realize that this world has been visited from outer space? But it was the Lord Jesus Christ who came, wasn't it? He came into the world to save sinners. And then Paul added, "of whom I am chief." It's as if Paul said, "If you were to line up all sinners from the greatest to the least, I'd be up front leading the band—the worst of the lot. Jesus Christ came into the world for the express purpose of saving me and my fellow sinners.

First John 4:14 says God sent Him into the world "as Savior of the world." First John 3:8 says, "He who sins is of the devil, for the devil has sinned from the beginning. For this purpose the Son of God was manifested, that He might destroy the works of the devil." He came to save all people; not just white people; not just rich people; not just poor people. Red and yellow, black and white, they're all precious in His sight. And friends, Jesus' coming into this world to be our Savior was not something we earned or deserved, was it? It was a matter of the grace of God Almighty. We did not deserve it; we did not merit it. But in spite of all of that, God sent His Son as a gift of His grace. And without the grace of God—please listen so you won't misunderstand me—without the grace of God, none of us can be saved, period! As one preacher of another generation would say, "That's not about it, that's it!" Oh, thank God we have a Savior!

Eternal Savior

We have a Savior right now who inhabits eternity. In John 8:58 Jesus said, "Before Abraham was, I am." He's talking about His eternal existence. There has never been a time when Jesus did not exist. The idea that Jesus was a created being is not Bible. Colossians 1:17 says, "And He is before all things, and in Him all things consist." The word *consist* means to uphold. He is the one who is upholding the universe this very minute. He is the one who's upholding this little ol' ball that you and I are living on, the one that's spinning around out here in space.

There's a prophecy about his eternal nature:

> But you, Bethlehem Ephratah, though you are little among the thousands of Judah, yet out of you shall come forth to Me the One to be Ruler in Israel, whose goings forth are from old, from everlasting (Micah 5:2).

Do you know what that means? Jesus inhabits eternity. He lives in eternity. No beginning, no end. Oh, what a Savior! Oh, what a Savior!

Born of a Virgin

We have a virgin-born Savior. His birth was divinely predicted. Isaiah prophesied, "Behold, the virgin shall conceive and bear a Son, and shall call His name Immanuel" (Isaiah 7:14). Let's look at the fulfillment of that prophecy. Matthew says, "Behold, the virgin shall be with child, and bear a Son, and they shall call His name Immanuel, which is translated, 'God with us' " (1:23).

Virgin born. Born of woman. Conceived by the Holy Spirit without the seed of man. The birth of Christ, the coming forth out of His mother's womb, was a natural birth. The miraculous part of his journey was the conception. And Jesus Christ was that seed of woman (Galatians 4:4).

Savior of Perfection

We have a Savior who lived a perfect life. Look at 1 Peter 2:22: "Who committed no sin, nor was deceit found in His mouth." Consider also Hebrews 4:15: "We do not have a High Priest who cannot sympathize with our weaknesses, but was in all points tempted as we are, yet without sin." Jesus was tempted just like you and I are tempted. When someone tells me he's never been tempted, I say, "We're all tempted, so you have been. Not only that, you were tempted just now to tell a falsehood, and you yielded." The difference in us and Jesus is when Jesus was tempted, He didn't yield. He lived a perfect life.

Jesus Christ's life of perfection was foreshadowed in the sacrifices of the Old Testament. You remember when the children of Israel were still in Egypt and the plagues came. The last plague was the death of the firstborn. To avert the disaster, Moses instructed the elders of Israel to find lambs "according to your families, and kill the Passover lamb" (Exodus 12:21). The lamb, less than a year old, was to be without blemish, that is, as near perfect as possible. Each family was to kill its lamb and put its blood on the lintel and doorposts of the house.

The Lord told Malachi to rebuke His people for offering blemished sacrifices—animals that were blind and torn and sick. Paraphrasing Malachi 1:8, the prophet said, "Why don't you try offering those things to your governor, and see if your governor will accept them at your hand?" God wasn't going to accept anything less than the best. And when it came to the offering of a sacrifice for the sins of the world, He offered the very best. He offered a perfect sacrifice.

Knowing that you were not redeemed with corruptible things, like silver and gold, from your aimless conduct received by tradition from your fathers, but with the precious blood of Christ, as of a lamb without blemish and without spot (1 Peter 1:18–19).

There was no blemish or spot in the Son of God, so He was qualified to be the perfect sacrifice for the sins of the world. Oh, what a Savior!

Our Savior Delivers Us

Friends, we have a Savior who died that we might live. Galatians 1:4 tells us He "gave Himself for our sins, that He might deliver us from this present evil age." And don't we need delivering from this present evil age? That's why Jesus died on that cross.

Think with me briefly about the events leading up to the cross. Consider His experience in the garden of Gethsemane. There was His betrayal by one of His friends. There was the trial all night long. Then the scourging, the crown of thorns on His brow. And then His trek to Calvary, knowing the pain that waited Him there. He was not alone on Execution Hill. Two others, one on either side, died with Him. Someone has said that on that day one man died in sin, the impenitent thief; one man died to sin, the penitent thief; and one man, the one hanging on the center cross, died for sin.

Picture Him with the nails in His hands, dying on that cross. They mocked Him; they spat on Him; they ridiculed Him. Then darkness covered the land from the sixth to the ninth hour. At the ninth hour He prayed to His Father, "My God, my God, why have You forsaken me?" (Matthew 27:46). He was forsaken by His own Father as He was hanging on that cross. That was the only time in all of human history that the Godhead was separated. And finally Jesus gave up the ghost. Jesus said, "It is finished." Oh, what a Savior!

Our Savior Lives!

Go to the Mosque of the Prophet in Medina, Saudi Arabia, and you can see Mohammad's tomb—he's still there. If you could find the burial place of Moses—he's still there. Go to the tomb of David—he's still there. Go to the grave of Mary Baker Eddy—she's still there. Go to the grave of John the Baptist—he's still there. Go to the grave of Alexander Campbell—he's still there. Go to the tomb of Jesus—He is not there! *He is risen!*

Paul wrote in Ephesians 1:19–20, "According to the working of His mighty power, which He worked in Christ when He raised him from the dead." We have a Savior who is alive. He is our contemporary. Hebrews 7:25 says, "He always lives to make intercession for them." Oh, what a Savior!

Friends, you have a Savior who is still in the business of saving souls. He can take a life that has been wrecked with sin—alcohol, drugs, or most anything—and fix it. Do you realize what He can do with you? He can make you whole again. He can make a new person out of you.

Someone says, "Well, how is He able to do that?" Because He is the one who said, "I am the way, the truth, and the life" (John 14:6). His is the source of life for us. In John 10:10 Jesus says, "I have come that they may have life, and that they may have it more abundantly." Jesus can give you a new life. Paul said, "If anyone is in Christ, he is a new creation, old things have passed away; behold, all things have become new" (2 Corinthians 5:17). He can help you put the old life behind and make a new man, a new woman, or a new boy or girl out of you. You'll be a new person in Jesus Christ. He and He alone can do that. Oh, what a Savior!

Salvation Now

And here is the beauty of His power: He can save you right now. He shed His blood that our sins might be cleansed—washed away. Listen to Him in Matthew 26:28: "For this is My blood of the new covenant, which is shed for many for the remission of sins."

One of our beloved hymns asks, "What can wash away my sins?" That's the question. Think about it for a moment. Think about this part of it: what can "wash away"? What does that mean? It means to eradicate, to eliminate, to cleanse, to wash away.

Now look at the next word: "my." What can wash away "my" sin? We're not talking about Abraham, are we? We're not talking about Moses. We're not talking about the penitent thief on the cross. We're not talking about Mama or Daddy or Grandma or Grandpa. We're talking about sins we've committed. What can wash away my personal sins? The answer to that question is found in Revelation 1:5, "To Him who loved us and washed us from our sins in His own blood." That's how our sins are washed away—in the precious blood of the Lord Jesus Christ. And we benefit from that blood when we put Christ on in baptism. As a penitent, confessing believer, we're buried with Christ in baptism. We're baptized into His death where He shed His blood. Baptism is an act of faith. I can assure you, there is no power in that water—no magic there. It's just plain ol' water. The power is human faith reaching for, and combining with, God's grace.

Examine Romans 6 before we finish this study. Too many religious folks today are making things up, and I want you to know I'm not doing that. Romans 6:3 says, "Do you not know that as many of us as were baptized into Christ Jesus were baptized into His death?" When we're baptized, God puts us into Christ. By faith, that's where we come in contact with His death—the benefits of His death—where He shed His blood (John 19:34).

> Therefore we were buried with Him through baptism into death, that just as Christ was raised from the dead by the glory of the Father, even so we also should walk in newness of life (Romans 6:4).

Isn't that what you want right now—a new life? Read the above passage again. Doesn't it tell you how to get that new life? And our Savior is the one who can give that to you. What we have to do is put our trust in Him. We must stop trusting ourselves and put ourselves in his hands. This is not a time for excuses, folks. It is not a time for us to be neutral, but it is a time for us to lovingly accept Jesus the Savior. Kneel at the foot of the cross.

Have you done that? Maybe this is the first time you've heard this from the Bible. But if you see what you need to do, please put your life in His hands. You know, you can put a basketball in my hand, and that basketball would be worth about nineteen dollars. You can put that same basketball in the hand of Michael Jordan, and it's worth 433 million dollars. The ball's value depends on who has it. You can put a baseball in my hand and that baseball would be worth about 6 dollars. But you put that baseball in the hand of Mark McGwire, and it's going to be worth 19 million. Put a wooden stick in my hand and I might be able to drive cows from the barn lot, but put a wooden stick in the hand of Moses and he can part a sea. Put some nails in my hands, you might get a birdhouse if you wait long enough, but put nails in the hands of Jesus, and He has the potential to save the world. It just depends on whose hands those nails are in.

Put your life in those nail-scarred hands today, won't you? Oh, what a Savior!

13

Were You There
When They Crucified My Lord?

We come to Calvary, the place where one Man died that all might live; the place where one Man died for sin that all might die to sin; the place where one Man was disgraced that all might be saved by grace.

Imagine Jesus hanging upon the old rugged cross and a jeering, mocking crowd surrounding Him. See them as they ridicule the Son of God. Watch as they spit on Him, slap Him, and blaspheme Him.

Before becoming critical and censorious of the angry mob, consider this question, "Were you there when they crucified my Lord?" Those same sins that drove the nails through Jesus' flesh almost two thousand years ago are still very much at work today.

There are five words in the title of this lesson that deserve emphasis. They are "crucified," "Lord," "there," "they," and "you." As we focus on these five words, five questions will be raised in an effort to answer the question: Were you there when they crucified my Lord?

Crucified

The word "crucified" tells what was done at Golgotha. Death by crucifixion was of ancient origin.

The earliest mode seems to have been by impalation, the transfixion of the body lengthwise and crosswise by sharpened stakes, a mode of death—punishment still well known among the Mongol race.

It was customary for the condemned man to carry his own cross from the flogging post to the site of the crucifixion outside the city walls. He was usually naked, unless this was prohibited by local customs.

At the site of execution, the victim was given a bitter drink of wine mixed with myrrh as a mild analgesic. The victim was then thrown to the ground on his back with his arms outstretched along the crossbar called the *patibulum*. The hands could be nailed or tied to the crossbar, but nailing was preferred by the Romans. After both arms were fixed to the crossbar, the patibulum and the victim were lifted onto the *stipes*—the upright post. Next, the feet were fixed to the cross either by nails or ropes. After the nailing, the *titulus* was attached to the cross just above the victim's head.

The victim usually survived from three hours to four days, depending upon the severity of the scourging.

Lord

The word "Lord" tells of the one who was crucified in our stead—the promised Messiah, the hope of mankind. Isaiah had the Lord's death on the cross in mind when he wrote,

> Surely He has borne our griefs and carried our sorrows; yet we esteemed Him stricken, smitten by God, and afflicted. But He was wounded for our transgressions, He was bruised for our iniquities; the chastisement for our peace was upon Him, and by His stripes we are healed (Isaiah 53:4–5).

Also, the one who was crucified was the sinless Son of God. Jesus' death on the cross was foreshadowed by the sacrificial system in the Old Testament. When the Passover was instituted, the Jews were commanded to take a lamb without blemish and put its blood on the two side posts and the upper doorposts of their houses (Exodus 12:5–7). Jesus Christ was God's perfect Lamb whose blood was shed for the salvation of the whole human race (1 Peter 1:18–19).

Furthermore, the one who died on the cross was one of the Godhead. On the first Pentecost after Jesus' resurrection, Peter declared to the very ones who had crucified Jesus: "Therefore let all the house of Israel know assuredly that God has made this Jesus, whom you crucified, both Lord and Christ"

(Acts 2:36). There were three crosses at Calvary, and the Son of God died upon one of them. He was God "manifested in the flesh" (1 Timothy 3:16).

There

The title of this study asks, "Were you *there* when they crucified my Lord?" Where was Jesus crucified?

Jesus was crucified at the place of a skull. "And He, bearing His cross, went out to a place called the Place of a Skull, which is called in Hebrew, Golgotha" (John 19:17).

One scholar observed: "It is very likely that the place of the Lord's crucifixion was called Golgotha, that is, the place of a skull, because of its skull-like shape, or perhaps because of the skulls scattered in that place in ancient time."

Again he said, "It might be noted that the word Calvary comes to us through the Latin version and the term is not an English equivalent for the New Testament original Greek word."

John writes, "The place where Jesus was crucified was near the city" (John 19:20). Jesus suffered outside the gate (Hebrews 13:10–14). This indicates the reproach and contempt He endured as our sin-bearer.

> There is a green hill far away
> Without a city wall
> Where the dear Lord was crucified
> Who died to save us all.
>   —Cecil Frances Alexander

"Now in the place where He was crucified there was a garden" (John 19:41). Later, Mary mistook Jesus to be the gardener (John 20:15).

They

The question, "Were you there when *they* crucified my Lord?" Human nature remains much the same through the years. It is significant that one may find, among the characters of the Bible, representatives of all the various types of people among us today. Such is true of those whose lives in some fashion touched the life of our blessed Lord. One may indeed discover among those who participated in the crucifixion individuals possessing the same attributes and characteristics, and reacting in the same manner we react today. Humanity, in outline, gathered at the foot of the cross.

- *The religious leaders were there.* Their hearts were filled with malice and hate because Jesus had uncovered their hypocrisy and laid bare their corrupt worship practices (Mark 15:10; John 19:11). They believed that if Jesus were allowed to continue His work, they would lose control over the people. These are the ones who had cried at His trial, "Away with Him, crucify Him." So as He was dying, they mocked Him: "He saved others; Himself He cannot save"; "Let Him now come down from the cross, and we will believe Him" (John 19:15; Mark 15:31; Matthew 27:42). They wanted religion but not a Redeemer. They wanted a Savior without a cross. In our day we have those who are religious but have no room for Jesus in their lives.

- *The bloodthirsty mob was there.* Four days before His death the people were singing praises to Him: "Hosanna to the Son of David! Blessed is He who comes in the name of the Lord! Hosanna in the highest!" (Matthew 21:9) Later that week those same people were shouting, "Let Him be crucified" . . . "His blood be on us and on our children" (Matthew 27:23–25). How do we account for the sudden change in attitude toward the Christ? Their leaders, by using untruths and deception, turned the once friendly people into an angry mob.

- *The pagan soldiers were there* (John 19:23). Those men had nothing against Jesus. They were obeying orders. Those rough pagans were accustomed to driving the nails through the hands and feet of criminals. To them the crucifixion of Jesus was just a job, and their job had created callous hearts within them. They could kill without thinking about it. Life was cheap, brutal, and meaningless.

The Roman centurion was in command of a hundred soldiers. Sometimes he received execution orders. But there was something different about the Man on the middle cross. When Jesus died, the veil that separated the Holy Place from the Most Holy Place was torn from top to bottom (Matthew 27:51).

As the earthquake shook the city at the moment Jesus died, the centurion felt there had been a miscarriage of justice in the death of this godlike person. He cried, "Truly this was the Son of God!" (Matthew 27:54). Despite the fact that he confessed the truth, we have no record of His further response to Christ.

- *Simon of Cyrene was there.* He was conscripted to bear the cross after Jesus (Mark 15:21; Luke 23:26). This man, who at first served unwillingly, gave two sons to the cause of the Lord (Mark 15:21).

- *Peter was at the cross.* He followed "at a distance" (Matthew 26:56–75). Later, Peter, in speaking for all the apostles, said concerning Jesus' death, "We are His witnesses to these things" (Acts 5:32). Peter was there on the fringe of the crowd.

   Perhaps he purposed to be far enough back so as not to be held responsible for the cause for which he had fled, nevertheless close enough that if anything happened, he would be on hand to enjoy it.

- *Women were at the cross:* the godly women who had followed Him from Galilee remained nearby to do what they could (John 19:25).

You

The question in the song for which this lecture is named asks, "Were *you* there when they crucified my Lord?"

We are so far removed from that day it is easy for us to say what we would and would not have done had we been there. A Prussian general once said: "If I had been there with my army, they would not have crucified my Lord." Is it not possible that we would have been among those who cried out for Jesus' execution or, at least, have been an indifferent witness?

In our day, don't we see the same kind of persons and conduct that were present when Jesus was nailed to the cross? In a figurative sense we were there! Somebody represented you; somebody represented me.

Is it not the case that we have in the world a pagan society, a counterpart to the soldiers who treated life so cheaply? Are there not those who regress to the level of beasts in their inhumanity to man?

Do we not have religious leaders who have no room for the one who died on Golgotha? They have no room for the doctrine of Christ (2 John 9–11). Even as the religious leaders in Jesus' day led the people astray, there are leaders now who are blind guides leading the blind. Such should be marked and avoided (Romans 16:17–18). Like the blood-thirsty mob that turned against Jesus, some even now will not be saved because they have allowed the misrepresentations and falsehoods of so-called religious teachers to blind their eyes so they cannot see the truth (Matthew 13:10–15).

Conclusion

There are those who are like the centurion. They acknowledge the truth, but like the centurion, they never do anything about it. They know the truth but refuse to obey it (2 Thessalonians 1:7–9).

Many are like Simon, who at first was not a willing disciple, but after carrying the cross for Jesus, took up his own cross and followed him (Matthew 16:24).

Sad but true, there are those like Peter who follow at a distance. Like the people of Laodicea, they are neither hot nor cold (Revelation 3:14–20). They cannot enjoy themselves at church because they yearn for the world. They cannot enjoy the world because of the goading of their consciences.

Happily, there are many like the women who put the church first in their lives (Matthew 6:33).

> Not she with traitorous kiss
> Her Savior stung.
> Not she denied Him with unholy tongue.
> But she, while apostles shrank
> Did dangers brave;
> Last at the cross, and first
> At the grave!
> —Selected

All humanity was present at the cross. It was there that Jesus died for everyone (2 Corinthians 5:21). He was thinking of you and me when He died (Hebrews 2:9). Yes, the most important fact in all of human history is that "God so loved the world that He gave His only begotten Son" (John 3:16).

The question is, "Were you there when they crucified my Lord?" Yes, you were there in a representative sense. Among those who gathered around the cross, there was someone who represented each of us. May we ever remember that it was upon the cross of Calvary that Jesus died for your sins and mine. He had us in mind when He climbed the bloody slopes of Calvary (Galatians 2:20). Since Jesus died for us, we ought to live for Him (Philippians 1:21).

14

I Love the Lord

Psalm 116 opens with this bold declaration: "I love the Lord." "Thou shalt love the Lord thy God" is the greatest and first commandment (Matthew 22:37 KJV). In the Old Testament God's people were told to love Him (Deuteronomy 6:5). Why should we love him? Psalm 116 presents some logical reasons.

1. *I should love the Lord because He hears me.* "Because He has inclined His ear to me, therefore I will call upon Him as long as I live" (Psalm 116:2). When the children of God call upon Him, He never turns away. He bends down in condescending love and listens. A woman once called me to discuss her broken marriage. After meeting with her, I encouraged her to get her children, as well as herself, back into Sunday school and worship.

   "Brother Lambert, I don't believe God would hear me if I prayed to Him," she said sadly.

   I replied, "I want to challenge you to get off by yourself and ask God to strike you dead."

   She gave me a quick, strange look. "I can't do that because I am afraid He would do it."

   I responded, "Let us analyze what you have just said. You think if you ask God for help He will not listen, but if you ask Him to strike you dead He will do it. I want you to know that is not the God of the Bible."

   That's a strange predicament for a Christian to be in, isn't it? Yes, I love the Lord because when I call upon Him, He hears me.

2. *I should love the Lord because He cares for me.* "Return to your rest. O my soul, for the Lord has dealt bountifully with you" (Psalm 116:7). I can cast all my cares upon Him because He is concerned about me (1 Peter 5:7). Years ago I made up my mind not to take my worries to bed. God is going to be up all night anyway, so why should I stay awake too.

3. *I should love the Lord because He delivers me.* "For You have delivered my soul from death, my eyes from tears, and my feet from falling" (Psalm 116:8). It is through Jesus Christ that we are delivered from the law of sin and death (Romans 8:1–2). He delivers us from tears in sowing to joy in reaping (Psalm 126:5). He wipes away all tears (Revelation 7:17). He holds us up when we are incapable of doing that for ourselves (2 Corinthians 12:9; Psalm 46:1; Jude 24). Yes, yes, I love the Lord.

How to Show My Love

It is unimaginable that anyone would fail to recognize God as the giver of all good things.

1. *I can show my love for the Lord by being aware of His benefits.* "What shall I render to the Lord for all His benefits toward me?" (Psalm 116:12). "Bless the Lord, O my soul, and forget not all His benefits" (Psalm 103:2). Throughout history people have tended to forget God and His benefits (Deuteronomy 6:12; 8:18). "Can a virgin forget her ornaments, or a bride her attire? Yet My people have forgotten Me days without number" (Jeremiah 2:32).

Stop and think about what God has given us. "Every good gift and every perfect gift is from above, and comes down from the Father of light, with whom there is no variation or shadow of turning" (James 1:17). Some gifts are good but may not be perfect. There are our families, our health, our freedom, and our jobs are good gifts, but they are not perfect. Then there are perfect gifts such as God's Son (1 Peter 1:18–19; Hebrews 4:15; 1 Peter 2:21–22) and the Bible (James 1:25). I recall hearing the late Willard Willis preach a sermon entitled "The Perfect Church." In it he pointed out that on the human side the church is imperfect, but on God's side it is perfect. The church is one of those perfect gifts of God.

The psalmist posed a question: "What shall I render to the Lord for all His benefits toward me?" (Psalm 116:12). The word *render* means to give, to consecrate, to dedicate. We should give, dedicate, and consecrate our all to Him (Romans 12:1–2). My time, influence, and yes, even the money in my possession are His. Like the magnificent Macedonians, we should first give ourselves to the Lord (2 Corinthians 8:5).

2. *I can show my love for the Lord by keeping my word.* "I will pay my vows to the Lord now in the presence of all His people" (Psalm 116:14, 18). Solomon taught that vows should be taken seriously. "When you make a vow to God, do not delay to pay it; for He has no pleasure in fools. Pay what you have vowed—better not to vow than to vow and not pay" (Ecclesiastes 5:4–5). The day you married you vowed to live with your spouse until death separated you (Matthew 19:6; Romans 7:2). When you borrow money you are promising (vowing) to pay it back (Romans 12:17). When you are called to testify in a court of law, you promise (vow) to tell the truth (Colossians 3:8). The day you confessed the name of Christ (Matthew 10:32–33) you promised to follow Him, to be loyal and faithful. We show our love for the Lord by keeping our promises to Him.

3. *I can show my love for the Lord by worshiping Him.* "I will offer to You the sacrifice of thanksgiving, and will call upon the name of the Lord" (Psalm 116:17). "I will pay my vows to the Lord now in the presence of all His people. In the courts of the Lord's house, in the midst of you, O Jerusalem" (Psalm 116:18–19). Why do we worship Him? We worship the Lord out of a heart of love. Why do we spend countless hours hunting, fishing, golfing, watching sporting events, and watching television in general? We do those things because we love to engage in the activities. We worship the Lord for the same reason. Once we understand we are in God's presence when we assemble

to worship, the human dimension of the church will be forever changed (Isaiah 6:1–8; Revelation 4:3–11; 19:1–10).

Three solid reasons have been established as to why we should love the Lord: (1) because He hears us; (2) because He cares for us; and (3) because He delivers us. Three ways have been shown as to how we show that love: (1) by recognizing God's benefits or blessings; (2) by keeping our promises; and (3) by never failing to worship Him.

The Glorious Future

"Precious in the sight of the Lord is the death of His saints" (Psalm 116:15). When we stand over the body of a loved one to deposit it into the earth, it is difficult to think of death as being precious. So why does the psalmist refer to the death of saints as precious? Because they have been delivered from the trouble, pain, and suffering of this world (Romans 8:18; Isaiah 57:1). The death of a Christian is also precious because it means the end of wearisome toil (Revelation 14:13).

Perhaps the most plausible reason the death of a saint is precious in God's sight is because it is a home-going. "We are confident, yes, well pleased rather to be absent from the body and to be present with the Lord" (2 Corinthians 5:8). At death our body is placed in the earth to await the final resurrection (John 5:28–29). Our spirit enters the realm of the disembodied spirits (Luke 23:43; 16:19–31; 2 Corinthians 12:1–4), paradise, to await the Lord's return. Then those who have loved the Lord will enter into the heavenly abode prepared for them.

> Let not your heart be troubled; you believe in God, believe also in Me. In My Father's house are many mansions; if it were not so, I would have told you. I go to prepare a place for you. And if I go and prepare a place for you, I will come again and receive you to Myself; that where I am, there ye may be also (John 14:1–3).

You are urged to show your love for the Lord by obeying the gospel of Christ. Believe on Jesus (Mark 16:16); repent of sin (Acts 3:19); confess faith in Christ (Acts 8:37) and be baptized into Christ (Romans 6:3–4) for the remissions of your sins (Acts 2:38). Jesus said, "If you love Me, keep My commandments" (John 14:15).

15

Summer Has Ended

"The harvest is past, the summer is ended, and we are not saved!" (Jeremiah 8:20). In Jeremiah's day, God's people were in a rather depressed state. Nebuchadnezzar's Chaldean army had Jerusalem under siege. They had been expecting deliverance but none came. Thus they cried, "The harvest is past, the summer is ended, and we are not saved!"

Summer and harvest are fit seasons for action. This is the time for the army to take the field, subdue the enemy, and bring about the deliverance of an oppressed people. The winter that follows is not a time fit for action. The words, "the harvest is past, the summer is ended, and we are not saved," are descriptive of those having trifled away all the gracious opportunities of life. They are found at the close of life, unforgiven and unprepared to meet God.

Someday
Summer is a time when children play and have no thought about tomorrow. Then one day the summer comes to a close. The summer of life is the time when many intend to change their lives for the better—to give more attention to spiritual things. That is the time of which some of us speak when we say, "One day I'm going lose a little weight." Or perhaps we make a spiritual commitment: "I am going to give my life to the Lord—someday." But then—the summer ends. Oh, you had intended to be baptized, you had intended to start reading your Bible, you had intended to meet regularly with the church for worship. But the summer has ended.

What is your life? "It is even a vapor that appears for a little time and then vanishes away" (James 4:14). If we would die the death of a Christian, we must live the life of a Christian. William Cullen Bryan said,

> So live when thy summons comes to join
> The innumerable caravan that moves
> To that mysterious realm, where each shall take
> His chamber in the silent halls of death,
> Go thou not like the quarry-slave at night,
> Scourged to his dungeon, but, sustained and soothed
> By unfaltering trust, approach thy grave
> Like the one who wraps the drapery of his couch
> About him and then lies down to pleasant dreams.

We should so live in the summer of life that when it comes our time to quit the walks of men, all will be well with our souls.

Time for Obedience

The summer of life is the time of golden opportunity. It is the time of opportunity for youth. What a great time to obey God! The truth is, if you do not obey God in the days of your youth, you may never obey Him. Solomon said, "Remember now your Creator in the days of your youth" (Ecclesiastes 12:1).

The days of your youth is the time to be baptized. Parents often ask, "Do you think my son or daughter is old enough to be baptized?" I do not know the age for a person to be baptized. Do you? He should be old enough to believe in Jesus. Unless he believes that Jesus is the Son of God, he cannot be saved according to John 8:24. He has to be old enough to have sins of which to repent. The Bible says, "Unless you repent you will all likewise perish" (Luke 13:3). A person has to be old enough to confess faith in Jesus Christ (Matthew 10:32–33). So if he is old enough to believe, repent, and confess his faith in Christ, and understand the significance of these things, he is old enough to be baptized. I do not think it has as much to do with age as with maturity and understanding. The days of youth are the days to obey God and give Him the best years of your life.

Time for Purity

Young people are to live a life of purity. Paul told Timothy to keep himself pure (1 Timothy 5:22). Paul's thinking is counter to the world's thinking. A speech about purity in contemporary society is as out of place as a hoop skirt in a fashion show. Christians must march to the tune of a different drummer. Keep yourself pure.

Time for Honor

In the summer of life you have the opportunity to obey your mother and father. And here is something every young person needs to know. You are not always going to have your mother and dad. If you are not in subjection to them, your insolence toward them will come back to haunt you after they are gone. The Bible says, "Children, obey your parents in the Lord, for this is right" (Ephesians 6:1–2). Now is the only time you have to do that.

Time for Example-Setting

The summer of life is the time for the young person to set a good example before others. Paul told Timothy, "Be an example to the believers" (1 Timothy 4:12). Show other people what it really means to live the Christian life. Some young people may say, "I know that is right and one day I am going to settle down and live my life for the Lord. But, you know, I want to have a good time first." Brother, you may sow your wild oats, but you are going to reap the wild oats. You may sow to the wind but you will reap a whirlwind.

> A young boy was a little on the mischievous side and his daddy punished him. The boy was to hammer a nail into the barn door every time he did something wrong. It was not long until the barn door was full of nails. Then his daddy said, "Every time you do something good you can take one out." It was not long before all the nails were out of the door. So his daddy congratulated him because his conduct had improved. The boy replied, "I know, Daddy, all the nails are gone, but the holes are still there."

You may think you are supposed to sow wild oats while you are young because, "When I get a little older, if I do get older, then I will settle down and live for the Lord." But the marks will be unpleasant memories and consequences. The holes and scars will still be there.

Time of Opportunity for Husbands

The Bible says, "Husbands, love your wives, just as Christ also loved the church" (Ephesians 5:25). That is a pretty big statement. What kind of love is that?

1. *Unselfish love.* Jesus gave everything He had for the church, even His life's blood. That is unselfish love. If I love my wife as Jesus loved the church, I am going to love her with an unselfish love.

2. *Sacrificial love.* Jesus gave Himself for the church. He did not give one of the angels to die for us; He gave Himself. Does that mean you have to die for your wife? I will tell you what it does mean. It means that in the great scheme of things, your wife needs to be in the forefront of your interest. You need to protect her, sacrifice for her, and love her no matter the cost.

3. *Pure love.* Heed the following description:

   > That He might sanctify and cleanse her with the washing of water by the word, that He might present her to Himself a glorious church, not having spot or wrinkle or any such thing, but that she should be holy and without blemish (Ephesians 5:26).

   That is a pure love. If you really love your wife, you will never do anything to contaminate that relationship. If you really love her, you will never do anything to allow anyone to come between you and the wife of your youth.

4. *Nourishing love.* A few years ago my wife and I went to Freed-Hardeman University where I spoke in a summer series. We stayed in a dormitory. A bird's nest rested snuggly in a small bush outside our window. We watched with keen interest as the mother fed her babies. One night a terrible thunderstorm came. I expected to find those little birds drowned next morning. But they were not. Do you know why? When the storm came, their mother cov-

ered them with her wings. This is the kind of love you should have for your wife.

5. *Unbreakable love.* "For this reason a man shall leave his father and mother and be joined to his wife, and the two shall become one flesh" (Ephesians 5:31). Jesus said, "What God has joined together, let not man separate" (Matthew 19:6).

> Several years ago I was preaching in a gospel meeting in Georgia. A man approached me with a problem one night after worship. He and his wife were divorced. The man was crying his eyes out. He said, "Brother Lambert, I did everything I knew to do for her." He told me how much money he made at his regular job. He also had a second job. Then he told me how much money he had in the bank and how much equity was in their house. He went on and on about the things he had done for her. I began thinking that he had spent so much time gathering "stuff" that he probably did not have much time for his wife. I wish now I had told him he did not give his wife the one thing she needed most. He did not give her himself. She wanted him more than she wanted his second job. She wanted him more than she wanted all the stuff he had worked so hard to get.

Give yourself to your wife. Why is now the only time that you have to do that? Someday death will separate you and your wife. I have seen men weep because they were not the kind of husbands they knew they could have been.

Time of Opportunity for Wives

Now is also the golden opportunity for wives. Ephesians 5:22 says, "Wives, submit to your own husbands, as to the Lord." The Bible teaches that wives are to be in submission to their husbands just like they are to the Lord. Someone may say, "I am not going to be submissive to any man." Once I quoted a secular humanist: "Nobody up there is going to tell me what to do." One of the students became irate because she had just told her husband, "No man is going to tell me what to do." If a man starts to act like a lord and dictator in the home, then he is not pleasing the Lord. He needs to straighten up his act.

However, a woman is to submit lovingly to her husband's leadership, just as he is to be the leader, provider, and protector of the home.

A fellow once told me he was the head of his house. In fact, he was way ahead of the house when she had a rolling pin in her hand. That is not what I am talking about. Another fellow told me, "I am the head, but my wife is the neck that makes the head turn."

Those illustrations reflect on the relationship between Jesus and the church. We are not the neck that makes the head turn. The wife should not be the neck that makes the head turn. She is to be submissive to her husband.

A Better Relationship

Kindness is the key to a better relationship. In describing a good woman in Proverbs 31:26, the writer says, "On her tongue is the law of kindness."

Have you ever considered that whatever we send out comes back to us? How will your life be different if you take the following two examples to heart?

Example #1: The Angry Echo

A little boy was reprimanded by his mother. He became angry, ran outside into the valley, and shouted, "I hate you! I hate you! I hate you!" The echo came back, "I hate you! I hate you! I hate you!" That frightened him so he ran back into the house, exclaiming, "Mother there is a little boy in the valley who said he hated me!" Mother knew what had happened so she suggested he return and say, "I love you, I love you, I love you." He did and that echo was much more encouraging than the first.

Example #2: Hurting Your Husband

A woman told a marriage counselor, "I want to hurt my husband. I don't like him; he irritates me, and I want to hurt him bad."

The counselor suggested, "I can help with that. For the next thirty days, do everything you know he likes. Prepare his special meals. Take his slippers, coffee or tea, and the newspaper to his recliner. Do everything you know he enjoys. After you have done that for thirty days, leave him. That will really hurt him." The unloved wife loved the idea.

Several weeks later the counselor saw the woman in a supermarket. He asked, "I'm sure you have left your husband, so how is your new life?"

She said, "Left him? No! And I won't! He's the most wonderful man I have ever known."

What she sent out came back. And so it is with us.

Time of Opportunity for Parents

Now is the time of opportunity for parents. You have the responsibility for the moral, ethical, and spiritual training of your children. Moses told Israel,

> Hear, O Israel: The Lord our God, the Lord is one! You shall love the Lord your God with all your heart, with all your soul, and with all your strength. And these words which I command you today shall be in your heart. You shall teach them diligently to your children, and shall talk of them when you sit in your house, when you walk by the way, when you lie down, and when you rise up. You shall bind them as a sign on your hand, and they shall be as frontlets between your eyes. You shall write them on the doorposts of your house and on your gates (Deuteronomy 6:4–9).

Let's talk a minute about rearing children. What are we to teach our children?

1. *Teach them to fear God.* One of the first things they need to learn is about God.

2. *Teach them to love God with all of their hearts.*

3. *Teach them the word of God.* Moses said, "These words which I command you today shall be in your heart" (Deuteronomy 6:6). After it is in your heart, you can teach it to your children. It is difficult to teach what you do not know. It is a grave mistake to neglect the word of God in the rearing of our children.

4. *Teach them by the minute, by the day.* The word of God in the routine of life, not only in some structured environment. Teach it when you lie down and when you rise up,

when you come and when you leave, when you sit down to eat supper and when you get up, and even when the children are getting dressed for school. When you are on vacation or doing things together, teach them about God. Teach them so when they exit your house to be on their own, they will love God.

Right now is the time of opportunity. They are small and pliable like clay. You can mold and channel them. David said in Psalm 127:4, "Like arrows in the hand of a warrior, so are the children of one's youth." We can give them direction when they are young.

I planted a little peach tree last spring. It is as small as a finger and bowed over. I drove a stake for support, but for some reason I have not had time to tie the peach tree to the stake. If I do not do it pretty soon, it is going to stay bowed over when it gets larger. If you do not begin training your children when they are young, you will never be able to guide them.

You can make an imprint of your palm in wet concrete. You can even print your name and the date on it. Try doing that thirty-six hours after the concrete has been poured. Impossible! Why? The concrete has hardened. It is the same with children. They are easily impressed when they are young. The older they become, the more difficult it is to make an impressions for good on their hearts. Do it while they are young.

Time of Opportunity for the Church

Now is the time for Christians to do all we can, for as many as we can, and for as long as we can. Now is the time to help others with their physical needs. I am happy to be a part of a congregation that cares about others. Galatians 6:10 says, "As we have opportunity, let us do good to all, especially to those who are of the household of faith." Many hungry folks are around us. Children who go to bed hungry are in our communities. Perhaps their daddies spent their paychecks on alcohol or their mommas spent family money on riverboat casinos. But the children have to pay a terrible price; they go hungry. We need to help those who are hungry or otherwise in bad circumstances.

Mostly though, we need to help people with their spiritual needs. We need to care. Some of the saddest words in the Bible are in Psalm 142:4. There David said, "No one cares for my soul." David was running from Saul, hiding in a cave.

I can imagine him as he looks around in that cold, dark cave. He felt so alone that he said, "No one cares for my soul." I do not want anyone we could have helped to have to stand before the judgment and say, "But Lord, no one cared for my soul." Caring for someone's soul requires deep conviction as to the existence of the soul. Genesis 2:7 says, "The Lord God formed man of the dust of the ground, and breathed into his nostrils the breath of life; and man became a living being."

Caring for a man's soul involves a conviction as to the value of it. To appreciate that, read the crucifixion of Jesus in Matthew 27. He was crucified because of His love for souls. Caring for souls involves a conviction of the danger to which a man's soul is exposed. In Matthew 10:28 Jesus said, "Do not fear those who kill the body but cannot kill the soul. But rather fear Him who is able to destroy both soul and body in hell." People can be lost.

> Two neighbors were at odds with one another. One of them, during a brief stop the country store, remarked to the storekeeper, "I'm going to get my shotgun and kill that man."
>
> The storekeeper told his son to run and warn the neighbor. The boy ran as fast as he could, but he had to stop for a breather. When resting, he saw a bird in the tree, so he picked up a rock, threw it, hit the bird, and killed it. When he went to pick it up, he remembered his mission, so he started to run again. As he came to a clearing near the man's house, he heard a shot; he was too late.
>
> "Did you warn him?" his father later asked.
>
> "No, Dad. He killed him."
>
> "What's on your hand, son?"
>
> "It's the blood of a bird. I stopped to rest, and I killed it while I was waiting."
>
> The father's uttered a plaintive response: "The blood on your hand is not the bird's blood. It's the blood of our neighbor."

The only time we have to reach men with the gospel is right now—in the summer of life.

Time of Opportunity for the Unsaved

The summer of life is an opportunity for the unsaved to put Christ on in baptism. Men can die outside the grace of God, and they often do. But that is unnecessary because the door of salvation is always open.

I read a story about a German family that devised an unusual means of execution. The one to be executed was put into a very ordinary-looking room. But after a few days, the walls began to close in on him. The room continued to shrink slowly until the very life was crushed out of the prisoner.

As I read that story, I thought, "What would a prisoner have done if there had been a small opening in the wall? And what if someone had opened the door just about the time space was running out? Do you think he would have said, "I don't know, I may do it tomorrow or on the second stanza of the invitation song. I need to have some time to think about it." Only a foolish man would do that!

The walls of eternity are closing in on all of us. Jesus is saying, "Come to Me, all you who labor and are heavy laden, and I will give you rest" (Matt. 11:28). The door is open now, but it will not always be. I plead with you with all the love in my heart to come now in the summer of life.

Summer Sowing

The summer sowing determines the fall harvest. Paul said, "Whatever a man sows, that he will also reap" (Galatians 6:7). We are going to reap what we sow in life. That is true agriculturally and spiritually. You cannot sow one thing and reap another. You are not going to sow watermelon seed and reap turnips. The kind of seed you sow is the kind of fruit you will get. You cannot sow bad seed and get good fruit.

Also, you are going to reap more than you sow. I cannot imagine a gardener planting one seed and expecting one seed in return. In that case, planting would have no purpose. From one seed planted the gardener hopes to get hundreds or thousands in return. If you sow only one seed, whether it is good or bad, there may be hundreds or thousands of the same kind. You reap more than you sow and a lot longer than you sow. A scoundrel may go to a convenience store, pull out a gun, and kill the clerk. That murder may take only a few seconds, but the murderer is going to reap a lot longer. The seed he sowed in the store will produce results in this life, as well as in eternity.

Make Preparation for Harvest

We need to make preparations. The summer is ended and the harvest is coming. What doctor would perform an operation without first making preparations? I do not want one "ad-libbing" through my body. I want someone who knows what needs to be done and is prepared to do it. What captain would go to sea without first making preparation? What pilot would allow passengers aboard without first filing a flight plan? Yet there are a countless number of unprepared people on their way to an endless eternity.

Paul was in prison when he wrote to Timothy: "Come before winter" (2 Timothy 4:21). He wanted Timothy to come to him before freezing winds and rains closed the ports. He wanted him to come while he had the opportunity. My plea to you is to come to Christ "before winter." Come while the door is open. Come while you have the opportunity.

Learn from the ant. Solomon said,

> Go to the ant, you sluggard! Consider her ways and be wise, which, having no captain, overseer or ruler, provides her supplies in the summer, and gathers her food in the harvest (Proverbs 6:6–8).

You probably have heard the following fable about the ant and the grasshopper.

> In the summer while the ant was preparing for winter, the grasshopper fiddled, danced, and played. When the winter came, the grasshopper was freezing and hungry. He came knocking on the door of the ant: "Let me in! Let me in!" The ant quietly said, "While I was preparing for winter, you fiddled, danced, and played. Now it is too late."

The time to prepare is now.

16

The Sufficiency
of God's Grace

And he said to me, "My grace is sufficient for you, for My
strength is made perfect in weakness." Therefore most gladly
I will rather boast in my infirmities, that the power of Christ
may rest upon me (2 Corinthians 12:9).

To fully appreciate this verse we must look at its back-
ground. In verse 2, Paul made mention of a man, who fourteen
years earlier was caught up into the third heaven or paradise.
Many believe Paul was referring to himself. If so, Paul had
been the companion of God.

After the glory came the pain. Paul also stated, "There was
given to me a thorn in the flesh" (2 Corinthians 12:7 KJV). The
word "thorn" (*skolops*) originally denoted anything pointed,
such as a stake. Paul's language indicates that the thorn was
physical, painful, and humiliating. W. E. Vine says this thorn
was also the "effect of divinely permitted satanic antagonism."
Sometimes criminals were impaled upon a sharp stake. "It
was a stake like that, that Paul felt was twisting in his body"
(William Barclay, 2 Corinthians, p. 257).

There are numerous ideas as to the true meaning of Paul's
"thorn in the flesh." Some see it as a spiritual temptation, maybe
the temptation to shirk his apostolic duty. Others see it as
opposition he faced in preaching the gospel. Still others see
the thorn as some carnal temptation. It has also been suggested that the thorn was a reference to Paul's physical appearance (2 Corinthians 10:10). Others say Paul was plagued

with epilepsy. Another theory is that Paul had recurring head-aches. Some think it was eye trouble (Galatians 4:15; 6:11).

Whatever Paul's thorn was, it is certain that God did not remove it. Three times Paul prayed for its removal and God's answer to his prayers was, "My grace is sufficient for you" (2 Corinthians 12:9).

What Is Grace?

What do we mean by the word grace? A common defini-tion is "God's unmerited favor." That is true. It is the favor God bestows that we do not earn or merit. Another definition is God giving man what man needs, rather than what man de-serves. And that is true.

Look at David, a well-known Old Testament king. David committed adultery. As a result, he committed murder. Accord-ing to Jewish law, David deserved to die. He said, " 'I have sinned against the Lord.' And Nathan said to David, 'The Lord also has put away your sin' " (2 Samuel 12:13) What did God do for David? He forgave him instead of taking his life. That is grace.

Another definition of grace is God doing for man what man cannot do for himself. That is equally true. Think about the expression "My grace is sufficient." Sufficient for what? The grace of God is sufficient to save us from our sins.

Grace for the Good, Bad, and Ugly

In his letter to the Ephesians, Paul wrote, "For by grace you have been saved through faith, and that not of yourselves; it is the gift of God, not of works, lest anyone should boast" (Ephesians 2:8–9). We can apply this passage in many ways. One application is this: some are saved and some are lost. Those who are lost are condemned because of their sins. "All have sinned and fall short of the glory of God" (Romans 3:23).

A couple committed a heinous crime. They were sentenced to die by hanging. As they waited in jail, the sound of the saws and the ring of the hammers across the street served as con-stant reminders that a gallows was under construction. Men without Jesus are eternally condemned. Almost two thousand years ago, though we did not deserve it or do anything to earn it, God sent His Son as the Savior into the world (1 John 4:14).

And, oh, what a Savior He is!

Jesus Christ came into the world to save sinners of all kinds, even murderers. Someone may ask, "Did you mean to say murderers?" Exactly. In Acts 2, on the day of Pentecost, Peter preached to a multitude whose hands were still red with the blood of Jesus. Peter said, "You have taken by lawless hands, have crucified, and put to death" the Son of God (Acts 2:23). Yet there were some three thousand saved that day (Acts 2:41). Jesus Christ came into the world to communicate with immoral people, the kinds of people that some of us would rather ignore. He came to save them!

In 1 Corinthians 6:9 Paul writes, "Do you not know that the unrighteous will not inherit the kingdom of God?" Then he continues by listing different sins, among which are adultery and homosexuality. But read verse 11: "And such were some of you." In the past, you may have been committing those kinds of sins, but what are you now? You are "washed," "sanctified," and "justified." So Jesus came to save immoral people.

He also came to save good moral people—upright, honest, sincere—like Cornelius (cf. Acts 10). He came to save them. When the Lord saves us from our sins, He does not do it half way. He thoroughly saves. The Bible has many examples. "As far as the east is from the west, so far has He removed our transgressions from us" (Psalm 103:12). God says in Hebrews 8:12, "I will be merciful to their unrighteousness, and their sins and their lawless deeds I will remember no more." When God forgives, God forgets. "Repent therefore and be converted, that your sins may be blotted out" (Acts 3:19). Our sins are blotted out. Remember the old ink blotters you used when you wrote with a fountain pen? You used the ink blotter to get rid of excess ink. When the Lord forgives our sins, He blots them out.

> A school teacher worked at a chalkboard, teaching math to a group of small children. She solved a problem, rubbed it off, solved another, and rubbed it off. A pupil, chin in his hands and elbows resting on his desk, was watching her every move. *I've finally gotten through to this little fellow,* she thought. Then she asked the class, "Do you have any questions?"

One little fellow raised his hand and said, "Teacher, where do them numbers go when you rub them off?"

Those numbers were gone. Similarly, when God removes our sins they are gone. He does not do a job half way.

Divine Longsuffering

Someone may ask, "Well, Billy, how does God's grace save us?" There is not a better illustration anywhere than in the Old Testament event of Noah and the flood. It was during the days of Noah that God saw that the world was very, very wicked. In the same way God sees that the world is wicked today. Finally, God said enough is enough; the end is come. But Noah "found grace in the eyes of the Lord" (Genesis 6:8). God commanded Noah to build an ark so he and his family were saved.

> When once the Divine longsuffering waited in the days of Noah, while the ark was being prepared, in which a few, that is, eight souls, were saved through water (1 Peter 3:20).

> Now look in Hebrews 11:7. By faith Noah, being divinely warned of things not yet seen, moved with godly fear, prepared an ark for the saving of his household . . . and became heir of the righteousness which is according to faith.

In both verses Noah is said to be saved by God's grace and his faith in God. But was Noah saved only by his faith in God? No.

In Genesis 6:22 we read, "Thus Noah did; according to all that God commanded him, so he did." How was Noah saved? By grace though the obedience of faith in God. Noah did not save himself. For Noah to have saved himself, he would have had to know a flood was coming, that an ark would deliver him, and how to construct a ship so large modern shipbuilders did not match its size until the late nineteenth century, less than 150 years ago! But he did not know a flood was coming and he did not know how to build the ark until God told him. But had Noah, in some way, foreseen all the flood and prepared an ark, he would have survived the flood and said, "Look what I did!" But the fact is, without God's revelation he could not have known to prepare. Noah was saved by the grace of God.

Consider the following illustration.

> Imagine a man walking across a field at night. In the darkness he falls into a hole. He had some experience that gave him an edge over others, so, at last, he was able to get out of the hole. Then he thinks, *Someone else may come along and fall in this hole, and he might not know how to escape. And, I don't have the means of filling the hole.* So he takes out a sheet of paper and writes simple escape instructions. He wraps the instructions around a rock, ties a string around the rock, and throws it into the hole.
>
> Soon another hiker tumbles into the same hole. He tries to get out by himself, but to no avail. Finally, he sees the rock with the instructions around it. He reads the instructions and follows them carefully. In a matter of minutes, he is out of the hole.
>
> Did he save himself? No! He was saved by the favor of the first man, the *unmerited* favor of the first man. The first man did not owe him anything. The first man saved himself and the second was saved by grace.

Bible Instructions

You and I were in the pit of sin. God looked down from heaven, and said, "Man cannot save himself; I must help him." So He sent His Son to die on the cross for our salvation. His Son died, was buried, arose, and ascended back to heaven. He instructed men to write salvation instructions. Those instructions are recorded in the Bible, and we are cleansed by the blood of Christ when we follow them. We are saved from our sins just like Noah was saved from the destruction of the world. That is, we are saved by grace through the obedience of faith.

Paul wrote to the Ephesians: "For by grace you have been saved through faith" (Ephesians 2:8). In the New Testament we learn what the Ephesians did to be saved by grace through faith.

1. *They heard the Word of truth.* "In Him you also trusted, after you heard the word of truth" (Ephesians 1:13). From this we can conclude that one must hear the truth in order to be saved by grace through faith.

2. *They believed.* "In whom also, having believed, you were sealed with the Holy Spirit of promise (Ephesians 1:13). This passage teaches very clearly that one cannot be saved by grace through faith without believing.

3. *They repented.* "Testifying to Jews, and also to Greeks, repentance toward God" (Acts 20:21). As evidence of their repentance, they burned their books of magic valued at fifty thousand pieces of silver (Acts 19:19).

4. *They confessed.* In speaking of the Ephesians, Paul said, "And many who had believed came confessing" (Acts 19:18).

5. *They were baptized.* "When they heard this, they were baptized in the name of the Lord Jesus" (Acts 19:5).

The grace of God teaches us how we are saved. "For the grace of God that brings salvation has appeared to all men, teaching us . . ." (Titus 2:11–12). What does the grace of God teach you? It teaches belief, repentance, and baptism. Consider these individually.

1. *The grace of God teaches us to believe.* In Acts 18:27 when Apollos was passing into Achaia, he "helped those who had believed though grace."

2. *The grace of God teaches us to repent of our sins.* Again in Titus 2:11–12, "The grace of God that brings salvation has appeared to all men, teaching us that, denying ungodliness and worldly lusts . . ." Is that not repentance? When we deny ungodliness and deny worldly lusts in our lives, is that not involved in repenting our sins? (Luke 13:3).

3. *The grace of God teaches us to be baptized.* "Not by works of righteousness which we have done, but according to His mercy He saved us, through the washing of regeneration and renewing of the Holy Spirit" (Titus 3:5).

In summary, we are saved by the grace of God when we believe in Christ, repent of our sins, and are baptized for the remission of those sins (Acts 2:38).

The Answer to Falling Is Standing

The grace of God is sufficient to save you. The grace of God is sufficient when His children sin. Christians are not perfect, are they? We are forgiven, but we can fall. Look at 1 Corinthians 10:12: "Therefore let him who thinks he stands take heed lest he fall."

Every time I hear that verse, I think of the time I was preaching at the old Fairview church in Wilmer, Alabama. On a particular Sunday morning I thought I had preached a fair sermon. As we were singing the invitation, I was making my way down the pulpit steps. I was not accustomed to that pulpit, and every preacher knows when you miss the top step, you will never get the second one. I sprawled out onto the floor. And yes, they laughed, but I did not think it was all that funny. I wanted to crawl out of the building on my hands and knees, but escape wasn't so easy. I had to face the crowd, so I stood up and said, "I have some scriptural advice for the next man in this pulpit: 'Let him who thinks he stands take heed lest he fall.' "

Someone may ask, "Well, can you fall from the grace of God?" Yes you can. Look at Galatians 5:4. "You who attempt to be justified by law; you have fallen from grace." Yes, you can fall away from the grace of God and you can fall out of favor with God.

But brethren, the answer to falling is standing. Look at Galatians 5:1. "Stand fast therefore in the liberty by which Christ has made us free, and do not be entangled again with a yoke of bondage." No, we are not perfect people, sometimes we err and fall away from the Lord. We may even drift away.

Grace Sufficient to Forgive

I do not know how your heart is today. It may be that you have become so discouraged that you have decided to just quit going to church. Maybe your heart is cold toward God, but I do know this. When God's children sin, His grace is sufficient to forgive us.

God's grace is the beautiful thing in the story of the prodigal son (Luke 15:11–32). The father in the story represents God. When the prodigal son came back home, the father fell on his neck, kissed him, and forgave him. Ours is a forgiving God. If you are a member of the church and need to come back home to the Lord, His grace is sufficient to forgive you.

Grace Sufficient for Trouble

Job said it best: "Man who is born of woman is of few days and full of trouble" (Job 14:1). Our world is filled with trouble and suffering. No person is exempt; not even a person like the apostle Paul (2 Corinthians 12:7–9; 4:8–10). He had trouble on "every side."

Many feel that way. Many suffer from physical pain. Others suffer from hunger, disease, war, and a thousand other things.

Perhaps you are suffering—silently suffering. What do you do? When your "thorn" becomes unbearable, what do you do? Where do you turn?

There is a word from the Lord: "My grace is sufficient" (2 Corinthians 12:9). In all the difficulties of life, God gives us the strength to endure and go on. "I can do all things through Christ who strengthens me" (Philippians 4:13).

Sufficient in Death

Go back with me almost two thousand years to a Roman prison cell. Paul is in that cell. The time of his execution has arrived and we ask him, "Paul, how do you feel right now?"

He would answer, "Well, I'll tell you, I am ready to be offered." Here are his exact words:

> For I am already being poured out as a drink offering, and the time of my departure is at hand. I have fought the good fight, I have finished the race, I have kept the faith. Finally, there is laid up for me the crown of righteousness, which the Lord, the righteous Judge, will give to me on that Day, and not to me only but also to all who have loved His appearing (2 Timothy 4:6–8).

How a man can come to the close of his life with that kind of spirit? By relying on the grace of Almighty God. It is tragic to come to the close of life alone. I cannot imagine it, can you? The most glorious thing you can ever imagine is to come down to the end of life, have all the forces of heaven around you, and be able to say with the psalmist, "Yea, though I walk through the valley of the shadow of death, I will fear no evil" (Psalm 23:4).

A young preacher sat beside a deathbed to console a sick man. "Just think of all of those wonderful things you've done for the Lord," the preacher said. "Think of all the good works you've done." Then he enumerated several of them.

The old man looked at him and said, "Son, none of that counts now. All that counts is the grace of God."

17

A Rainbow in the Cloud

And God said: "This is the sign of the covenant which I make between Me and you, and every living creature that is with you, for perpetual generations: I set My rainbow in the cloud, and it shall be for the sign of the covenant between Me and the earth. It shall be, when I bring a cloud over the earth, that the rainbow shall be seen in the cloud; and I will remember My covenant which is between Me and you and every living creature of all flesh; the waters shall never again become a flood to destroy all flesh. The rainbow shall be in the cloud, and I will look on it to remember the everlasting covenant between God and every living creature of all flesh that is on the earth" (Genesis 9:12–16).

That scripture reading takes us back to the days of Noah. After the flood, God made a promise never again to destroy the world with water. He sealed that promise with a rainbow.

A rainbow is an optical and meteorological phenomenon that causes a spectrum of light to appear in the sky when the sun shines onto droplets of moisture in the earth's atmosphere.

God told Noah that the rainbow would be in the cloud. In life, for every cloud there is a rainbow.

Ancient Concepts

To the Greeks, the rainbow was the path Iris traveled from the earth to heaven. The Persians connected the rainbow with the divine messenger. The Hindus have described the rainbow as a weapon in the hand of Indris with which he hurls flashing darts. The Chinese once believed the rainbow was a sign of forbearing trouble and misfortune.

The Rainbow Is a Symbol of God's Divine Presence

"There was a rainbow around the throne" (Revelation 4:3). "I saw still another mighty angel coming down from heaven, clothed with a cloud. And a rainbow was on his head" (Revelation 10:1).

The rainbow is a symbol of God's mercy (Ephesians 2:4; Psalm 51:1), and His mercy is "from everlasting to everlasting" (Psalm 103:17). The rainbow is also a symbol of hope. Many are asking, "Is there any hope?" The answer? Yes, there is. Jesus is our hope (1 Timothy 1:1). We are saved by hope (Romans 8:24).

Furthermore, the rainbow is a symbol of the unchanging nature of God's will (Matthew 24:35; 1 Peter 1:25). The rainbow was a promise to Noah that the earth would never again be destroyed by water. It is also significant that the rainbow symbolizes God's judgment upon the earth. Noah saw the rainbow after God destroyed the earth. Every time you see a rainbow, remember that God will destroy the world, not by water but by fire (2 Peter 3:10).

The Rainbow Comes Out of the Cloud

"The rainbow shall be in the cloud, and I will look on it to remember the everlasting covenant between God and every living creature of all flesh that is on the earth" (Genesis 9:16). Clouds come into our lives. As I write this, I am in the Great Smoky Mountains. A huge mountain is in the distance. I know because I saw it this morning. Now clouds obscure it from my view.

Think of the clouds that come into your life:

- *The cloud of guilt.* A man sent a check to the Internal Revenue Service. His conscience was bothering him; he felt guilty. Why? He had been cheating on his taxes. He included a brief note confessing his wrong. Then an addendum to the back of the note told the rest of the story: "If I still can't sleep at night, I'll send the rest."

    Guilt! That caused the Jews on Pentecost to inquire, "What shall we do?" (Acts 2:37).

- *The cloud of sorrow.* "Man who is born of woman is of few days and full of trouble" (Job 14:1). There is so much hurt and trouble in our world: hunger, disease, war, domestic trouble, misrepresentation, criticism, and hundreds of other things that cause sorrows.

- *The cloud of bereavement.* It hangs over the heads of all humanity. In my almost fifty years of preaching I have seen many tears shed, tears over wayward children, tears over an unfaithful spouse, tears over the loss of a loved one. David wept when his son Absalom died (2 Samuel 18:33). Godly women shed tears when Dorcas died (Acts 9:39). The church made great lamentation over Stephen's death (Acts 8:2). When Lazarus died, Jesus "groaned" in His spirit (John 11:33) and "wept" (John 11:35). Our youngest daughter died in the year 2000, twelve days after giving birth to a precious little girl named Callie Grace. Her son Caleb was twenty-three months old at the time. On July 15, 2009, little Caleb tragically died. I can tell you, the pain of losing loved ones hangs like a thick cloud over your life.

- *The cloud of cross-bearing.* The apostle Paul lived under that cloud (2 Corinthians 11:24–28). He suffered so much for Jesus' sake, I become ashamed when I think of how little I have suffered for His cause. Paul knew what it really meant to take up his cross and follow Jesus Christ (Matthew 16:24).

- *The cloud of conflict.* Conflict frequently comes our way (Philippians 1:30). It comes in many forms: misunderstanding, opposition, ridicule.

- *The cloud of earthly sojourn.* We earthlings who live in this thing called a body "groan" (2 Corinthians 5:4). Many things depress and discourage us, but thank God there is hope in the midst of the cloud.

Blessings from the Cloud

Rainbow of Pardon

Outside the cloud of guilt is the rainbow of pardon. Ours is a God who is willing to pardon abundantly (Isaiah 55:6–7). David sinned by committing adultery. Them he sinned again by conspiring to have his lover's husband killed. When confronted by a prophet, David exclaimed, "I have sinned." Nathan then told David the Lord had put away his sin (2 Samuel 12:13).

Please know and understand that if you live under the cloud of guilt, God wants to forgive you. When God forgives, He removes our sins as far as the east is from the west (Psalm 103:12). When we are willing to surrender to His terms of pardon—faith in Christ (John 8:24), repentance (Luke 13:3), confession of faith in Christ (Romans 10:9–10), and immersion into Christ in the waters of baptism (Colossians 2:12; Romans 6:3–4; Acts 2:38)—our sins will be washed away in the blood of the Lamb (Revelation 1:5; Acts 22:16).

Rainbow of Support

From the cloud of sorrow comes the rainbow of support. "Casting all your care upon Him, for He cares for you" (1 Peter 5:7). Why try to carry all your burdens when there is someone who will help you?

Rainbow of Reunion

It just gets better! Out of the cloud of bereavement there comes the rainbow of reunion. I have been asked many times, "Brother Lambert, do you think we will know one another in heaven?" I don't think we will—I know we will! In Luke 16 Abraham was still Abraham, Lazarus was still Lazarus, and the rich man was still the rich man. There is nothing in scriptures to indicate that we lose our identity when we die. In Matthew 17 Moses and Elijah appeared at Jesus' transfiguration. These men had been dead for hundreds of years, but Moses was still Moses and Elijah was still Elijah.

Will we know our loved ones? If not, why not? Why would we lose our identity? When King Saul tricked the witch of

Endor into calling up Samuel—and I must say that much to her surprise, Samuel came back—Samuel was still Samuel. Yes, out of the cloud of bereavement will come a happy reunion.

> But I do not want you to be ignorant, brethren, concerning those who have fallen asleep, lest you sorrow as others who have no hope. For if we believe that Jesus died and rose again, even so God will bring with Him those who sleep in Jesus. For this we say to you by the word of the Lord, that we who are alive and remain until the coming of the Lord will by no means precede those who are asleep. For the Lord Himself will descend from heaven with a shout, with the voice of an archangel, and with the trumpet of God. And the dead in Christ will rise first. Then we who are alive and remain shall be caught up together with them in the clouds to meet the Lord in the air. And thus we shall always be with the Lord. Therefore comfort one another with these words (1 Thessalonians 4:13–18).

There is a rainbow in the cloud.

Rainbow of Crown-Wearing

Additionally, from the cloud of cross-bearing will come the rainbow of crown-wearing. There is a crown of righteousness laid up for the faithful Christians (2 Timothy 4:8).

Rainbow of Victory

Also, out of the cloud of conflict will come the rainbow of victory. We can say with Paul, "Thanks be to God, who gives us the victory through our Lord Jesus Christ" (1 Corinthians 15:57).

Rainbow of a Heavenly Home

Finally, out of the cloud of our earthly journey comes the rainbow of our heavenly home. It was said of Abraham, "He waited for the city which has foundations, whose builder and maker is God" (Hebrews 11:10). Heaven is a wonderful place prepared for God's children (John 14:1–6). It is a place where there will be no tears, no death, no pain, no sorrow (Revelation 21:4).

You can believe it with all your heart. There is a rainbow in the cloud! Paul said it best in these words: "For I consider that the sufferings of this present time are not worthy to be compared with the glory which shall be revealed in us" (Romans 8:18).

Caleb's Sermon

Wearing Down Our Spiritual Life

Caleb Coxwell
June 3, 2009
(Caleb's notes as he wrote them)

When we are babtized, we feel we are ready to do anything, but with some of us that wears off. Well, think of a pencil. When you sharpen it you feel you can write the neatest, but the lead will soon wear down, then you have to sharpen it again. Well we shouldn't have to resharpen our spiritual life. Please turn in your Bibles to Matt. 5:14, 16. Ye are the light of the world, a city set on a hill cann't be hid let your light so shine before men that they may see your good works, and glorify your father which is in heaven. We have to stay sharpend all the time so people can see our spiritual light. What are some ways our spiritual life can wear down?

1 hearing dirty jokes
2 Bad music
3 Bad TV shows
4 Bad photos
5 Playing bad vidio games

What are some way we can keep our spiritual life sharpend?

1 reading the bible
2 Not speaking bad language
3 hearing clean jokes
4 watching good shows
5 Not seeing bad photos
6 Going to church all the time
7 Praying

Oh another thing about the pencil is the eraser. The eraser is like Jesus's blood, can erase our sins away. Turn in your

Bibles again to Rev. 1:5 and from Jesus Christ who is the faithful whitness, and the 1ˢᵗ begoten of the dead, and the prince of the kings of the Earth. Unto him that loved us, washed us from our sins in his own blood. That verse is saying that Jesus forgave us of our sins. Maybe your spiritual life has worn down and you need the prayers of the church or you want to be babtized you know in acts 22:16 it says and now why tarriest thou? arise and be babtized and wash away thy sins calling on the name of the Lord. So when we are babtized Jesus's blood washes away our sins.

If you need to come forward, come now why we stand and sing.

THANK YOU